Adventures in Faith

A Reflection on My Life in Africa

Nancy Warlick

Adventures in Faith
A Reflection on My Life in Africa

by Nancy Warlick

Signalman Publishing
www.signalmanpublishing.com
email: info@signalmanpublishing.com
Tampa, Florida

Scripture taken from The Message. Copyright© 1993, 1994, 1995, 1996, 2000, 2001, 2002. Used by permission of NavPress Publishing Group.

ISBN: 978-1-940145-89-1

Cover photo shows the author with Stanley, one of the first children to stay at the Kanyama Crisis Nursery. The batik shown was created by John Moyo.

Cover design by Joel Ramnaraine.

10-11

Printed in the United States of America

Dedication

To my husband Bill of nearly 59 years. Friends have used the label "the man, the myth, and the legend" to describe him. He's been made an honorary chief in both Ghana and Cameroon. He's my soul mate, my encourager, and my strong spiritual partner. Thank you for your unfailing support through our many adventures of faith.

To my grandchildren, Robert, Frances, Chloe, and Jack, who are a delight to Bill and me. May the Lord guide you in your own adventures in faith.

Nancy and Bill's Ministry in Africa

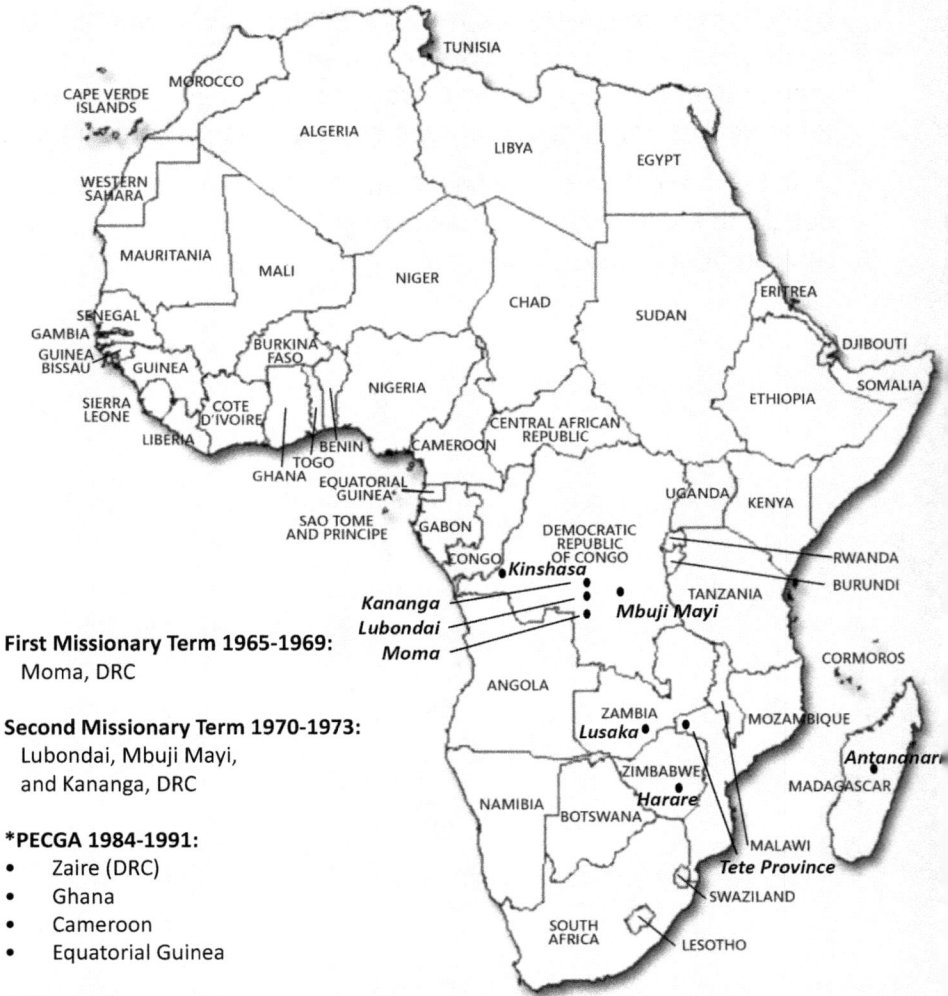

First Missionary Term 1965-1969:
  Moma, DRC

Second Missionary Term 1970-1973:
  Lubondai, Mbuji Mayi,
  and Kananga, DRC

*PECGA 1984-1991:
- Zaire (DRC)
- Ghana
- Cameroon
- Equatorial Guinea

*PECGA 1994-2014:
- Zimbabwe
- Zambia
- Malawi
- Mozambique
- Madagascar

* Project for Evangelism and Church Growth in Africa (PECGA)

Table of Contents

Foreword

Nancy's book is a journey in faith of a woman's love for God and love for the people of Africa. I first met Nancy and her husband, Bill, when they were commissioned as missionaries by the Presbyterian Church in Montreat, NC. I was a member of the Board of Trustees of The Outreach Foundation of the Presbyterian Church. The Warlicks were being called to Africa as evangelistic missionaries, and The Outreach Foundation Board's desire was to ensure our prayer and financial support for them. We continued that support during all the years they were on the field in Africa.

My wife and I made our first trip to Africa as a part of a delegation for a consultation with African leaders at Lake Munkamba, Democratic Republic of Congo. We marveled at the joyous interaction of the Warlicks with their African brothers and sisters in Christ. Their lives impacted our lives, and that trip changed the direction of our ministry. The Outreach Foundation's Executive Director position was open. I was pastor of First Presbyterian Church in Nashville, Tennessee. Nancy called me and said that she and Bill had been praying about the vacancy, and the Lord had laid it on their hearts to call me and ask me to consider it. That was the last thing I was going to do but I could not get it off my mind. Bette and my prayers joined Bill and Nancy's prayers, and when I submitted my name it was with more certainty and peace than I ever had known.

Through the years as Executive Director, I frequently invited people to journey with me to Africa to see what God was doing through the faithful witness of the saints. It was Nancy and Bill who ministered to us. Our group witnessed their commitment to the churches of Southern Africa to whom they pledged their lives. Together we saw them as they made their home and raised their family in a land often filled with famine and revolution. We marveled in their assurance of God's protective care. We rejoiced in their marriage as a partnership of two people with different gifts united in love and support. We shared their awesome challenge to be the body of

Christ to the world. We experienced their contagious excitement in sharing the love of Jesus. Most of all, we saw that love determine how they responded to things that happened, the people with whom they met and the way they treated those circumstances and those people.

I thank God that I have shared life with Bill and Nancy Warlick, and also with countless others who have been recipients of the love of Jesus through them.

Rev. Dr. Bill Bryant

Executive Director of the Outreach Foundation

1994 – 2002

Acknowledgements

The writing of this book has taken a long time, much longer than I expected. I would like to thank several special friends and family members who have helped me along the way. Sybil Shaw was the first friend who suggested that I write a book. Peen Hardy has spent hours of typing, editing, and helping me finish this project. She has traveled to Southern Africa with us on many Outreach Foundation trips. She has given me incredible feedback and has been my strong encourager through this whole process. Pam Bowman has been another strong supporter. She edited and proof-read the book and helped it take professional shape. Our daughter Elizabeth has been an invaluable help with the final editing stage of the book. Of course, she grew up in Congo and now works in Madagascar. It is thanks to her final editing efforts, as well as encouragement, that I have finally finished the book. Lastly, thanks to my husband Bill for his support, assistance, and patience.

Prologue:
Only Those with Clothes

Mozambique was considered the poorest country in the world in 1994. Much of the country had been devastated by thirty years of war, especially the last sixteen years of vicious civil war. Fighting and instability drove tens of thousands of people from their homes. Those Mozambicans living in Tete Province particularly lived in terror, often fleeing in the night, taking what little they could as they escaped into southern Malawi to live as refugees in makeshift camps. They would return home empty-handed to start life over, only to be driven away again by the violent acts perpetrated by rebel soldiers. Most families endured these migrations several times during the war years.

My husband, Bill, and I were not allowed to visit Tete Province as we had hoped in October 1994. Robbers and unexploded land mines alongside the main road made travel unsafe. By the following March, however, things had calmed down and we were determined to make the 450-mile drive from Harare, Zimbabwe, where we were living and working as Presbyterian missionaries. Our job was to coordinate the Project of Evangelism and Church Growth in five sub-Saharan countries: Zambia, Zimbabwe, Malawi, Madagascar and Mozambique. We had met with Presbyterian denominational leaders in the other four countries and were eager to meet the pastors, evangelists, and lay leaders in Mozambique.

Crossing country borders in Africa is stressful in the best of times. On this trip there were armed military police in charge of customs and immigration. We held our breath as they checked our car thoroughly for weapons or other contraband, and when we were given the go-ahead to enter Mozambique, we let out a sigh of relief, thanked God, and started our adventure.

During that first visit to Tete Province, the congregation at Ampande Presbyterian Church invited us to worship in the thatch-roofed church they had built. It was packed with men, women, and children, and those who couldn't squeeze inside peered through the windows or stood in the doorway. It was hard to understand what was said during the lively service, but we were moved by their warm welcome, and we felt the presence of God in the joyful dancing and singing.

Manuel Ostene Kambene, a young evangelist, spoke some English and translated for us. He had written a welcome skit and recruited several young people to act it out for the congregation. Hours later, when the worship service concluded, every single person wanted to shake our hands, from the smallest child to the oldest adult. Later Manuel told Bill, "There would have been even more people present, but only those who had clothes came." Until then, we had not realized fully the extent to which the Mozambicans had suffered as refugees, and that they still lacked basic necessities. In the days ahead we worshiped together with other congregations and wept over the poignant stories they shared. But we also saw how they turned to the Lord as life became more difficult and how they drew strength from God's word and his promises, living the words of Psalm 54:4: "The Lord is the one who sustains me."

In our subsequent visits to Tete during those early years after the civil war, we discovered that many Mozambicans had accepted Jesus Christ as their Savior when they heard the Good News from Malawian Presbyterians while they were in refugee camps in Malawi. The Church of Central African Presbyterian (CCAP) was one group that regularly held worship services and Bible studies in the camps. Refugees had suffered unspeakably, yet they became faithful and joyful Christians. Yeretsami Kamangeni is one such person. We will never forget him.

Yeretsami and his wife had thirteen children. The family fled many times into southern Malawi in the years between 1976 and 1992. Tragically, ten of their thirteen children died during that time. We could not begin to imagine such loss! Yet Yeretsami found Christ as his Savior in a refugee camp, and his faith remained strong. We found him to be a modern-day Job.

Yeretsami explained he knew that God understood his grief, because in John 3:16 he read that God loved the world, and loved *him* so much, that God sent His only son to die on the cross for him. When he and his wife returned to their village, Chimphako, with their three living children, he started a "prayer house" for worship and Bible study. Calling Christians together, they began meeting, first under a tree and then in a thatch-roofed stick church they built themselves. Then they began the tedious process of making bricks to build a permanent church building. We wondered why, while *they* still lived in mud huts, would the villagers put this great effort into constructing a permanent building for a church. "God has rescued us from death," they replied, "and we want to honor Him by building a proper church in which to worship Him." That was the first of several "prayer houses" started by Elder Yeretsami Kamangeni.

Henri J.M. Nouwen wrote that we learn more of who God is as we, the followers of Jesus, share our life stories together. Bill and I have heard haunting stories from our African sisters and brothers, stories that have both touched us and enriched us. We have worked, prayed, worshiped, and enjoyed fellowship with wonderful African Christians for almost fifty years. Their stories have taught us what it means to be obedient and faithful followers of Jesus Christ.

In his book *Lifesigns,* Nouwen speaks of Jesus' words in John 15:4: "Make your home in me as I make mine in you." Nouwen writes of the spiritual implications of homelessness and loneliness. Bill and I often marveled that countless thousands of homeless, needy Africans have found their home in following Jesus Christ. Church statisticians now say that almost half of the African continent—encompassing nearly a billion people—is Christian. It has been said that in times of turmoil, people are more open to the Gospel. We certainly found this to be true in Africa.

The Beginning

My love affair with Africa goes back a long way, but I'll get to that later. I was four years old when my mother said I accepted Jesus into my heart. I used to look at pictures of Jesus on the cross and cry.

I could be a difficult child at times, often sick, suffering from asthma and severe allergies to milk, eggs, butter, cheese and oranges, as well as dust, mold and grass. Doctors were not sure that I would survive childhood. There were times when knowing Jesus as my Lord and Savior was important in my life. There were other times when this knowledge didn't matter, and it didn't seem to change my headstrong behavior. I was fortunate to have a father, William Holt Wooddell, who loved and mentored me, and a very wise mother, Frances Kump Wooddell. She was a gifted teacher, a wonderful Christian, a prayer warrior, and filled with compassion. In addition, Mother was very interested in the mission field. We often had Presbyterian missionaries visit us in our home in Beverly, West Virginia. Years later, I learned that Mother had wanted to be a missionary and, although she did go to Africa when she was older to teach missionaries' children, she didn't get there as a young lady. But she prayed me onto the mission field; I know that.

I grew up in an interesting family in West Virginia. My father was a talented lawyer, a great storyteller and very charismatic. We moved from the state capital, Charleston, where Dad had served as assistant attorney general, to the small town of Beverly when I was four years old. There were three girls: Peggy, my older sister; Jane, my younger sister; and me in the middle. Our family home was full of history. It had been a hospital during the Civil War. During our twelve years in Beverly, we worshiped at the small Presbyterian church in the center of town. Being involved in the life of the church was an integral part of our family life.

Our home was close to Mother's family in Elkins, only six miles away. My grandfather, Herman Guy Kump, was a prominent lawyer and former governor of West Virginia. He and my grandmother, Edna Scott Kump, built a big house in Elkins where our large family gathered for many Sunday dinners after attending church. We also lived not too far from Dad's parents, William Lawrence Wooddell and Marguerite Miller Wooddell, in Webster Springs. "Papa" was what we called Dad's father. He was a caring lawyer who faithfully taught Sunday School in the Methodist church. "Nana" was his warm and loving wife. We enjoyed visiting them and hearing stories of their side of the family.

Standing with my parents in front of our house in Beverly, WV

As I got older, I admit to having had a temper, but at about ten years old, I had a life-changing encounter with Jesus. That day, in the middle of a temper tantrum, I was sent to my room. While there, I looked out of my window into our neighbor's yard and was drawn to a bright, dazzling, yellow-white light shining in their big oak tree. As I looked closer, I realized I was seeing the back of Jesus. He had his hand up, as if pointing to something that was up ahead. I was awestruck and speechless. I didn't want Him to turn around because I knew that I couldn't stand it if He did. However, I realized that He wanted to get my attention, to let me know He was there. I ran downstairs and told Mother what I had seen. She told me that if I had indeed seen Jesus, I had better go back upstairs to my room, get down on my knees and get right with Him. I do remember that my life was different after that experience. I felt calmer, less prone to outbursts of temper, and closer to the Lord.

**With my parents and sisters, Peggy (seated L)
and Jane (standing) in Elkins, WV 1955**

My twelfth summer I attended Pioneer Conference at Davis and Elkins College, a conference for junior high children that was sponsored by the Presbyterian Church. Mother's friend, Ethel Witherspoon, was the Bible teacher that week. We were studying Ephesians. I vividly remember one night around the campfire thinking that I had somehow been given an understanding of the book of Ephesians and had a familiarity with this book beyond what we were covering in the daily Bible study. During another night that week I heard God's voice saying to me, "I want you to serve me in the Belgian Congo." No one else heard the voice of course, but I was quite moved, and this experience shaped the direction of my life. The next morning, I talked to Mrs. Witherspoon about what had happened and how I was feeling. I told her, "All this week we've studied the book of Ephesians. I feel almost like I have prior knowledge of many passages in this book." She laughed and said, "Nancy, has your mother not told you that the summer she was carrying you, she was teaching a Bible study from the book of Ephesians at a Presbyterian Women's Synodical Training School? The women would laugh, point to her stomach and say, 'How is Little Ephesians?'" How incredible I thought, that even before I was born Mother was teaching the Word of God and somehow, by God's grace, it had connected with me in her womb. From that time on, I knew I was to go to the Belgian Congo.

This love affair with Africa is very real. I have fallen in love with the African people and particularly the precious African children. I remember that after God's call to me to be a missionary in Congo, I never really wanted to do anything else with my life. I went through both high school and college being called "the little pygmy" because I was only five feet tall, and because of my plans to go where pygmies live. It seems I was always preparing to go to Africa and serve on the mission field. Everyone knew this about me.

My family moved to Orlando, Florida, in March 1955. I remained behind to finish my senior year at Beverly High School. I was valedictorian of my senior class. There were only twelve of us! I chose to attend Southwestern-at-Memphis (now Rhodes College) because I knew one of the professors, Dr. Dan Rhodes, who had been my pastor in Beverly and had baptized me when I was ten years old. I also chose Southwestern to major in French. I wanted to prepare myself as best I could for serving in Congo where French is the official language, and that school had an excellent French department. Dr. and Mrs. Rhodes kindly invited me to stay with them the first semester of my freshman year, September 1955, but I moved into the dorm the second semester. French was my major, Latin my minor, and I worked as secretary of the French department. I made many wonderful friends during those four years and had some wonderful, dedicated professors. It was good preparation for the mission field.

On June 2, 1959, I graduated and was very surprised to receive the Algernon Sydney Sullivan Award, given for excellence of character and service to humanity. Each year the faculty chose a graduating student "who, because of the quality of their lives, are judged to be appropriate recipients of this distinction," and who are chosen because of philanthropic work in which they have been engaged during their time at the college. It was named for Algernon Sydney Sullivan (1826–1887), who "reached out with both hands in constant helpfulness to his fellow men." This honor has meant quite a lot to me over the years.

College Graduation

By the following summer in 1960 I was at Montreat, North Carolina, for six weeks of orientation and commissioning by the Presbyterian Church in the United States (PCUS) as a missionary. However, that was the year of Congo's independence from the colonial rule of Belgium; the Belgian Congo became the Democratic Republic of Congo. There was a lot of turmoil, violence, and political uncertainty in the country. As a result, Presbyterian missionary wives and children were sent back to the United States. I had planned to teach missionary children, but now they were all coming home. Dr. Darby Fulton, a man of God I deeply respected, was head of the Board of World Missions for the PCUS. He called me in while I was at Montreat to talk about the future. He said, "Nancy, as you know, you're not going to be able to go to Congo. I've got positions in Japan and in Brazil where you could go to teach missionary children. You can pray about this. But my word of advice to you is this: since you have prepared for so long to go to Congo, and you know God has called you there, you may want to go back and teach in Florida for a year and wait to see what happens in Congo." I knew he was a wise and wonderful Christian with a pastor's heart, so I took his advice and returned to Florida to teach 3rd grade for another year in Seminole County.

One incredibly special, life-changing event happened that same summer. While I was at the World Mission Conference in Montreat,

I met Bill Warlick, a rising senior at Columbia Theological Seminary in Decatur, Georgia. He swept me off my feet. We began dating and fell in love. He would drive down to Orlando as often as possible to see me. I was living with my parents and teaching third grade in Seminole County. In turn, I would visit Bill and stay with my sister Jane, a freshman at nearby Agnes Scott College.

Bill had a keen interest in serving as a missionary and had felt God's call in high school to go to Brazil. He applied to the Presbyterian Board of World Missions the summer of 1961 after finishing his Master of Divinity degree at Columbia Seminary. Dr. Watson Street, head of the Board of World Missions, told Bill he thought it would be good for him to take a church and have the experience of being a pastor in the U.S. before going overseas. Since Bill had a strong interest in Brazil and I still felt that God was calling me to Congo, we decided that this word from Dr. Street was sound counsel. However, Bill had an inkling he would eventually concede to my wishes as he felt "the cards were stacked" for us to go to Congo.

Bill and I were married on July 11, 1961, at Park Lake Presbyterian Church in Orlando. After a brief honeymoon, we went to live in Anniston, Alabama, where Bill had accepted a call to serve as associate pastor at the First Presbyterian Church, but with the job description to start a new congregation in the Golden Springs area of the city. This was a wonderful time for us. We loved beginning our married life

Bill and I were married at Park Lake Presbyterian Church in Orlando

together with the very special people who became members of the new Church of the Good Shepherd. Our two older children were born during this time, Elizabeth in 1962 and William, Jr. in 1964. This was also a turbulent time for race relations all over the country. Anniston was caught up in the racial violence. Bill was part of an interracial clergy group that met together, prayed, and took action to stand up against injustice. I supported them with prayer.

We had talked about going to Congo after three years, but we stayed in the U.S. an extra year because my dad had cancer and died in 1964. Another reason for our delay in leaving was that our church was in the midst of a building program, and we wanted to stay until its completion. We loved the beautiful new church sanctuary and were excited to worship in it for the first time on November 10, 1964. We thank God for giving us such an incredible congregation. It was very hard to leave our family and those we had come to know and love in Anniston.

Getting to Congo

At long last, we headed for the mission field in August of 1965. Elizabeth was three and William was one. We went by ship to Rotterdam and then by train to Brussels, Belgium, to study French and colonial history. I had majored in French, but Bill had studied Spanish in high school. He struggled with the French language and with being in Brussels for a year when he really wanted to be in Congo. Despite the harsh weather that winter, which I didn't like, I enjoyed the year more than Bill did. We were glad to have fellowship with other PCUS missionaries who were also there for language study. While in Brussels, Elizabeth attended a French-speaking kindergarten, and an older Belgian lady cared for William in our apartment when I was in class.

During this time, Joseph Mobutu came into power as president of Congo. We learned later that the U.S. government helped put him in this position. We all were praying that things would settle down in the country and that independence would bring a better quality of life for the Congolese people. Unfortunately, this didn't happen. Mobutu turned out to be a cruel dictator of terrible proportions.

We finally arrived in Kinshasa on July 18, 1966. We were assigned to live at Moma, a rural area near the Angolan border in West Kasai Province. We flew from Kinshasa to Luluaboug (now called Kananga) and spent a couple of days buying food and supplies before going on to Moma on a small mission plane. Bill wrote, "We arrived here on Saturday, July 23, 1966, with a warm welcome from the village and from missionaries: Charles Streshley; Dr. Arnold Poole; Mary and Paul Donaldson; and the Carper family—Day, Blanche, Janet, Elizabeth and Edie. We walked through the station and saw the middle school and high school, the dispensary, and part of the nearest village." We were assigned to live on the mission station in a spacious stone house, third in a row of houses built by earlier missionaries. Bill noted, "Not many Congolese live here on the station." The only Congolese living there were the two school directors and their families, and Reverend Bernard Kandau, the local Presbyterian pastor, and his family.

While it seemed like "the end of nowhere" to us, as I think back over our time at Moma, we did have three wonderful years. The mission station was surrounded by three small villages. We really bonded with the people living in the area, members of the Basala Mpasu tribe. Although French was the official language of Congo, not everyone spoke it here, so we began language study very soon in order to speak Tshiluba, one of the three major Bantu languages spoken in this part of Congo. Elizabeth and William were able to go freely into the villages nearby and had many friends. They learned Tshiluba effortlessly from their playmates, while Bill and I struggled to become fluent. During our middle year in Moma, our two were the only white children around, but that didn't matter. They felt right at home.

We soon learned quite a lot about the culture and customs of the local people. I was called "Ma Elizabeth" (the mother of Elizabeth) and "Ma William" (the mother of William). The Congolese people love children. I had "standing" because I had both a son and a daughter, although having a son gave me more prestige. It was a man's world there. We learned that the right hand was called *tshianza tshia balume* in Tshiluba, meaning "the hand of the man." It was more important than the left hand, *tshianza tshia bakaji,* or "the woman's hand." You were expected to wave, to receive a gift, and to shake hands with the right hand or with both hands, but never with the left.

We saw poverty like we had never seen before. Most of the rural people lived in thatched-roofed houses with dirt floors. Very few had access to electricity or clean, running water. Diseases such as malaria and tuberculosis abounded. Malnutrition was common. We never got used to seeing severely malnourished children.

Bill and I were fortunate to be in Africa when there was more medical help and knowledge, although in our early days in Congo there were not the effective medicines that came later. The early missionaries often had no idea what to do about dreaded diseases such as malaria, typhoid fever, etc. Within that first year Bill, Elizabeth, William and I all had malaria, and Bill even had cerebral malaria. Blanche Carper, a missionary nurse, treated Bill. He ran an extremely high fever and was in isolation. I don't think I realized at the time how sick he was, but God was gracious and Bill survived. Although we slept under mosquito nets and took weekly medicine to prevent malaria, the kids both contracted malaria and ran high fevers from time to time. We were very careful to stay inside in the evenings when the mosquitoes were out.

Malaria is a virulent disease. Even today there are a million deaths worldwide from malaria every year. Eighty percent of these deaths occur in Africa south of the Sahara. Malaria kills more people in Africa than any other disease, even HIV-AIDS. I am thankful that the Bill and Melinda Gates Foundation decided to focus on the diseases that are causing the most deaths in the world—malaria, TB, and HIV-AIDS, particularly in Africa where those diseases are rampant and where so many people are poor and suffer from malnutrition. Scientists are still working on a vaccination for malaria. Work that began years ago was slowed down or stopped because pharmaceutical companies thought it would not be a big moneymaker.

Mosquitoes weren't the only problem. We had to watch out for scorpions, fleas and other bugs as well. One of our worker's jobs was to clean and mop the floors and use spray disinfectant. Also, we checked our shoes and left them upside down at night to discourage scorpions or spiders from crawling into them. Sadly, Congolese children were often bitten by scorpions, and we knew of children in our area who had died from the poison.

Bill was assigned to be an evangelistic missionary working and itinerating with Congolese pastors and evangelists in the area. He often traveled with several pastors from rural areas. We came to appreciate and love our Congolese sisters and brothers in Christ and grew very close to many of them. I was asked to teach Bible in French to students in *Cycle d'Orientation*, the local Presbyterian school for junior high/middle school students. Every morning I would walk from my house to the school, which was nearby on the mission station. I was asked to teach two classes of Bible, each with thirty to forty pupils. It was a special time for me to learn more about the culture and life of these young people, as well as about their home situations and their thoughts and dreams. We had a lot of interaction. I had learned from my mother that studying the scriptures is an incredible way to learn more about yourself and about others, so as we studied a Bible passage, I'd ask my students what these verses said or meant to them. In this way we were able to talk freely about God and His Son Jesus Christ. They loved to act out the Bible stories. Pastor Kandau, our Congolese pastor, explained to me that most Congolese believe in God and believe that He created the world, but they did not totally understand that He is a God of love and that He sent His Son, Jesus, to die for their sins. They believed that after creation God went off somewhere and left the world in the hands of the forces of good and evil. There was always a struggle between these two forces. And yet at this time many Congolese were eager to hear about and receive the Good News, that God sent his only Son to live here on earth and to die for them in order that they might have eternal life.

As I learned just how hard life was for many of my African friends and for the young people I taught, I saw how they turned to God with their problems. They were able to understand that God was the one who created them and who knew them intimately. They could go to God with their concerns, pain and sorrows and He would give them the strength, the hope, and the courage to live for Him each day.

Meanwhile, Bill and I continued studying Tshiluba. It's not easy for Westerners to learn an African language. Although Bill will tell you that I probably have better linguistic skills than he, it was very challenging for both of us. We had to learn to think like the Africans and to see the world through "new eyes." It was humbling. Thankfully, we had an extremely helpful grammar book that was written by Virginia Pruitt, one of the earlier Presbyterian missionaries. The principal of the elementary school, Antoine Kabunda, was assigned to tutor Bill, and I had Beya Samuel, the principal of the high school, as my tutor. These two men became great friends of ours. We could exchange ideas with them and talk freely as we learned conversational Tshiluba. These two men helped us understand cultural differences and ways to be more culturally sensitive. We were all close to the same age and we decided early on that we would be open and honest with each other. Even when Bill or I had a touchy or delicate question, we felt we could ask them, and it was the same for them. We learned that it was culturally unacceptable for women to wear slacks or shorts. To be respectful, I never wore slacks or shorts in my three years at Moma. Antoine and Beya also shared with us that it was predominately a man's world in Africa, but that education helped to level the ground between the sexes. However, few Congolese girls had the opportunity to go very far in school at that time. God blessed us with these two men to be our friends and to orient us to life in the Congo. Years later we met Beya in Kananga and again in Kinshasa, but we never saw Antoine after we left Moma in June 1969.

Our relationship with Pastor Kandau and his wife was also special and taught us a great deal about cultural realities in the Congo, especially the different roles of Congolese women and men. A member of the Basala Mpasu tribe, Pastor Kandau had the pointed, filed front teeth typical of this tribe. The Basala Mpasu were formerly cannibals and were considered fearless by outsiders. He was a dedicated Christian, very committed to preaching the word of God and to Bible study and prayer. He wanted us to feel part of the Presbyterian congregation at Moma. After three or four months, he asked Bill to preach a sermon in Tshiluba during morning worship. Bill worked hard on his sermon and practiced giving it to Antoine, his tutor, so that he could be understood. It was only about fifteen or twenty minutes long. After Bill finished preaching that morning, Pastor Kandau asked the congregation to bow their heads and pray. During the prayer, he thanked God for the young visiting pastor's sermon and proceeded to give the main points of Bill's message. It was obvious that he didn't want anyone to miss what Bill had said.

We laughed later about this and were thankful that at least Pastor Kandau understood Bill and was able to relate the main points to his congregation.

Bill and I were the "new kids on the block," and Pastor Kandau enjoyed interacting with us. He was an interesting man with a great sense of humor. He particularly loved to get me thinking and talking, even debating Bible passages with him. He asked us many questions because he knew we had gone to college and Bill had gone to seminary. He said that he knew we'd been trained well and had a very privileged upbringing. Pastor Kandau loved our homemade peanut butter, and there were many times when he'd come to the house and we'd have either peanut butter sandwiches or peanut butter on crackers and then talk about scripture passages or about cultural differences. Or we'd go to his house to visit. He and I would talk, even spar, about women's roles. He loved to push my buttons.

About this time, Bill began to travel a lot so I would sometimes go alone to the pastor's house and visit with him and his wife. We'd have tea together and talk about what the Apostle Paul said about women. I enjoyed bringing up passages such as Galatians 3:28: "There is neither Jew nor Greek, slave nor free, male nor female, for all are one in Christ Jesus." But Pastor Kandau would say, "Yes, but women have a certain place in society, and they're supposed to know their role and stick to it. They're supposed to listen to their husbands and obey what their husbands say as the Bible tells us in Ephesians 5:22–26." I would bring up other verses such as "Husbands, love your wives … don't provoke your wives," and we would debate a bit more. His wife usually would stand behind him, cheering me on. He couldn't see her huge smile or hear her silent laughter as we continued our good-natured debating.

Those three years were good years for our family, learning about life in Congo and making many Congolese friends. As active members of the Presbyterian Church of Moma, we felt right at home in the church and in the community. Many times, I would sit and say to myself, "Yes, Lord, this is what you prepared me to do." And Bill felt the same way. We came to love the people and they came to love us.

We also enjoyed the fellowship of the older and wiser Presbyterian missionaries stationed at Moma: Day and Blanche Carper, who began service in 1940, and Bill and Ruth Metzel who began in 1949. The Carpers' three daughters and the Metzels' older three children all attended boarding school. The youngest Metzel, Daniel, was Elizabeth's age, and he became fast friends with our two. Day and Bill were seasoned pastors. They shared many of their experiences with my Bill and took him on some of his first road trips with Congolese pastors and evangelists. Once a year we had a missionary retreat, usually at Lake Munkamba where the PCUS had built a retreat center. This was a wonderful time for spiritual renewal and fellowship with other PCUS missionaries.

Me with William and Elizabeth in Moma

The years from 1966 to 1969 were also special for our children. In the mornings, I home-schooled Elizabeth, kindergarten and first grade, but the children had the afternoons free. There was an untouched forest area nearby, and William and Elizabeth would announce, "Mom, we're going to the jungle." I didn't worry about their safety since Congolese friends always went with them. Their jungle, in fact, was home to African gray parrots and other special birds as well as several monkeys. The kids just loved being able to wander freely. During those years Elizabeth and William would often be invited to eat at the homes of friends. They especially relished eating bedia, the staple food made of manioc flour. The Congolese eat bedia two or three times a day. Unfortunately, it doesn't have much nutritional value, but for many it is all they could afford. Elizabeth and William would leave our table in an instant if they had an invitation to eat with their friends. I vividly remember the day when William and his friends were out catching field mice. He announced, "This is what we're going to have for supper tonight!" I nearly lost it! My first inclination was to stop him, but Bill, who has always been a wise father, told me to let him go. I think, in fact, William did go that evening and eat those field mice. But when he came back and told us he had had a good supper, I thought, "OK, Lord, I hope he doesn't tell me what he ate and that you'll not let him get sick from whatever it was!" Elizabeth and William also ate insects, just as their Congolese friends did.

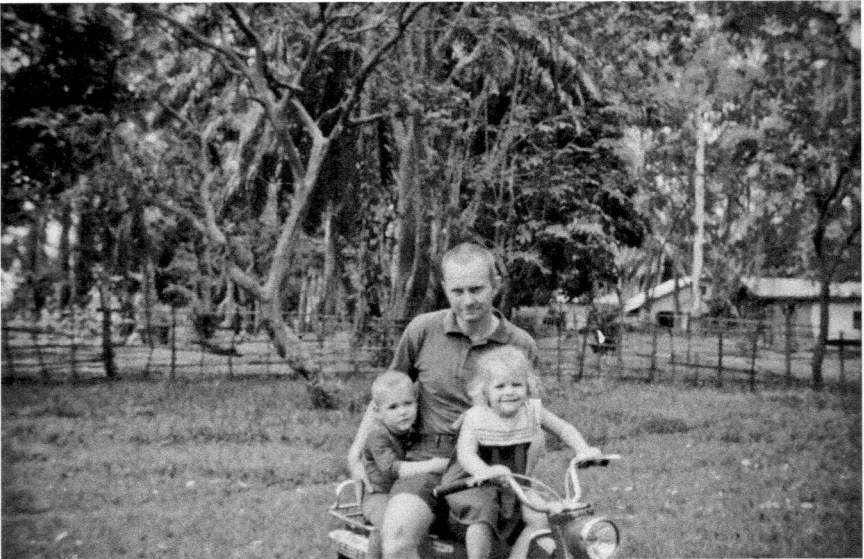

Bill with William and Elizabeth in Moma

My younger sister Jane came to teach for a year in 1966, and my mother came in 1967. They split a two-year term teaching missionary children at Central School in Lubondai, only about three or four hours away from Moma, and visited us on the holidays. We always loved having them as guests in our home. On one of Mother's visits, William ran outside saying, "Quick, the *nsua* (flying termites) are ready!" When the Congolese heard rumblings in the ground, they would put big palm leaves around the holes and catch these insects for eating. A lot of the Congolese people cook the termites before eating them, but the children would catch the insects, eat them on the spot, and spit out the wings. Mother said she went through extreme culture shock and nearly died when she walked out and saw her grandson eating flying termites and spitting out the wings. She came inside and said to me, "Do you know what your son is eating?" I answered, "Yes, Mother, he's done it several times." And I often had to remember that, after all, John the Baptist ate locusts and wild honey!

Although I didn't always enjoy it, there were many opportunities for Bill and me to eat unusual food. When we were invited out, it was appropriate to eat everything that was offered. Bill used to laugh about family night suppers in Africa and how different they were from the church suppers back in the U.S. We had to sample everything—flying ants, fish eyes, and grub worms. The Congolese love to eat grub worms, but I had to draw the line there. Several times when Bill was traveling with pastors, they would be served monkey. It was quite a delicacy and serving it was meant as an honor, but it bothered Bill because they would skin the monkey so that it looked very much like a small human child. But when monkey meat was offered, he accepted what they had prepared for him. Bill has a much stronger stomach than I do! There were many occasions when we knew that people were preparing for us, at great expense, the very best food they could find. We were humbled over and over again by their generosity.

Naturally during our years in Africa, we had several encounters with snakes. Since three out of five snakes found in Congo are poisonous, we saw many, many unusual and dangerous ones. When we lived at Moma we were in a rural area with lots of snakes, both green and black mambas, vipers and adders. Mambas are among the deadliest snakes in the world. Sometimes we found mambas on our station. They would jump from one huge palm tree to another.

There are those who think snakes don't jump, but we've seen it.

For Elizabeth's sixth birthday party we invited about twenty kids, although at least thirty or thirty-five showed up. We were playing games in the back yard, but when it got too warm, I suggested we move to the front yard where there were mango trees for shade. About thirty minutes later, someone screamed, *Nyoka!* (snake in Tshiluba). I ran to the back yard where the kids had just been playing and saw a pit viper slithering across the yard. What if the kids had been right there! That was a very sobering experience for me, but again I realized the Lord had protected us, and we had moved to the front yard before the snake came. One of our workers quickly killed the snake with a rock.

There were many other times when snakes were closer than any of us wanted. We had a CB radio in order to keep in daily contact with other missionaries and mission stations. The radio was housed in what we called the radio shack, and we locked the building at night. We had regular broadcasts at a set time after lunch each day, although if we had a special need to talk earlier or later to someone, or had a medical problem, we would make a date to speak at another time. One day when I went in for the broadcast, I looked up at the roof and saw what I thought was a green chameleon. I wasn't keen to be in there with a chameleon, so I lit out. As it turned out, what I saw was actually a green mamba. Someone (not me!) chased the snake away; we weren't able to kill it that time. Once again, the Lord's protection was felt!

Dr. Johnny Miller, a pediatric missionary doctor, was famous for being able to find and handle snakes. He had grown up in Congo and had always been passionate about them. The Congolese held him in high esteem because he collected live snakes. One time Bill, Elizabeth, William, and I were visiting Johnny and his wife, Aurie, in Bulape, where he was head doctor at a "bush" hospital. A mission plane was coming in to take Johnny on a village run to see some patients. We had finished lunch and went out on the porch where we discovered a snake curled up in the corner, looking like a bright green chameleon. One of the Congolese workers yelled "Nyoka!"

We stood at the door. Johnny confirmed that it was a green mamba and told us to move away. He called for his snake stick, a pronged stick. But whoever he called to bring it ran the other way—exactly what I would have done! Johnny finally captured the snake and put it in a metal milk container. He put the lid on, but the snake could lift the lid a little bit. Aurie told him, "You cannot leave the snake in that condition while you are gone. You need to get it secured." So before departing he found another place for the mamba!

The missionary kids were not as afraid of snakes as the adults, even though we told them the snakes were poisonous and warned them to report to us if they saw any snakes while they were outside chasing field mice or each other. The kids told us that when the parents made them wear shoes and take a flashlight at night, that's when they saw the snakes. During the day, when they were allowed to go barefoot and run free, they had no problems with snakes! I remember there was a missionary child at Lubondai who stepped on a snake one night and was bitten. We all prayed for him, for we knew of Congolese who were bitten by snakes and became gravely ill or died. Thankfully, he survived.

One year at Moma, Bill and I had the only refrigerator in the community. The antidote for the bite from a black or a green mamba came from South Africa and needed to be given within twenty-four hours of the snakebite. It was expensive and didn't keep well. Since we were in a very remote area and had no way to get that particular serum in an emergency, we kept antidotes and medicines for the clinic. We are thankful that our family didn't ever need it.

At missionary retreats on Lake Munkamba, where many missionaries had homes, we always heard great snake stories. Usually they came from Dr. Bill Rule, Dr. Johnny Miller, or Bill Pruitt. They were fascinating storytellers and had had many snake encounters. All three men were fearless!

Our children had a mongoose once as a pet while we were in Moma. Someone brought it when Bill was traveling, and I agreed to let the children keep it because I knew it would keep snakes away. William was about four at the time. He had a rocking horse on the front porch and decided he would give the mongoose a ride one day. Of course, this activity was not meant to be, and the mongoose slipped off and broke its neck. William and Elizabeth were very sad when the mongoose died. We had a funeral service to say goodbye.

During those first three years in Africa we had an almost idyllic situation because we were allowed to live in one place for the entire time; however, one year there were inconveniences and difficulties because Bill was gone on itineration with Congolese pastors and evangelists half the time. During our last year he was away two-thirds of the time. It seemed any family crisis would happen only when he was gone. We were able to communicate by CB radio, but no contact could be made when Bill was moving around. I remember one time William was sick with malaria, running a very high fever. Blanche Carper, a missionary nurse, was at Moma the first year, but during our second year we were the only foreigners or expatriates ("expats" for short) at Moma and had little or no medical care nearby. Every three weeks a Presbyterian missionary doctor—Walt Hull, Ken McGill, or sometimes Ralph Shannon—would come down to Moma to hold a clinic. We could call for medical help on the CB radio, but the radio wasn't always available. Bill and I prayed about whether to remain there that second year as the only missionaries on the station. It was a hard decision for us as neither of us had medical training, but the Lord let us know that He wanted us to be there, that He would take care of us and watch over our kids in any situation that might confront us.

In December 1968, we were invited by Catholic priests from a nearby mission station for a Christmas celebration. William and Elizabeth, who were four and six, were out playing on the grounds. There was a train track nearby and somehow William fell and cut his head quite severely. The skin was laid open and he was bleeding quite a lot. I prayed, "OK, Lord, you promised to take care of us!" A surgeon from Belgium was visiting the Catholic fathers. He stitched up the wound, and William was left with no scar. So again, God showed me, "When you step out and do what I ask you to do, I will keep my promises." And that was pretty amazing.

Another instance when we felt God's protection was when Elizabeth almost set herself and her brother on fire. The two children shared a room and slept under mosquito nets for malaria protection. They were scared of the dark, so we left a candle on their dresser with strict instructions never to touch the candle. Elizabeth was usually very good at obeying rules, but on that night, she wanted to read to her little brother in bed. So, she took the candle under her mosquito net in order to read to him. As you might predict, the mosquito net caught fire. William wanted to watch the flames, but Elizabeth realized the danger, grabbed William and ran to tell us! We were able to put the fire out, but it was a close call. When our hearts stopped racing, we gave thanks to God for his protection.

We truly felt we were where God wanted us to be. We were among incredible people who loved Jesus Christ. It was during that period (1966 to 1969 and into the '70s) that the church of Jesus Christ was growing dramatically in Africa, and the Congo the Presbyterian Church was gaining members. People were coming to accept Christ, and not just because we missionaries were there. Early missionaries had presented the Gospel and had helped to translate the Bible into the languages spoken by the people, and now Africans were telling each other about Jesus. I think of D.T. Niles' comment that evangelism is one beggar telling another beggar where to find bread. Those of us who are sinners and needy tell others about Jesus' love. I know that was what was happening in Congo and elsewhere in the African church.

We remember our time in Moma as a wonderful way to start our service in Congo and in Africa. Life was pretty relaxed since there were not many places to go, and we enjoyed having time to get to know our neighbors. We enjoyed being able to worship at the same church each week—at least the children and I did. Bill was often on the road. I didn't travel much because Elizabeth and William were young, and I was teaching them as well as conducting Bible classes for Congolese students. I didn't drive a car in the entire three years I lived there. We walked, gardened, and had picnics. Bill created a clever miniature golf course with tin cans and other available materials and taught the kids to play. He had a wonderful garden. Friday night was game night with the kids, and sometimes we invited the Congolese students from the Presbyterian school where I taught to join us in the games. We all read quite a bit. One year, Mother asked what she could send me, and I requested a subscription to the Sunday *New York Times*. Sometimes the paper took three or four months to get there, but I would pour over each issue. Life was simpler for us in the rural community, without the stresses and pressures that we encountered in urban areas. Hardly anyone owned a watch. (Africans say that Americans have the watches, but Africans have the time!)

However, it was while we were in Moma that I realized what hunger does to people, especially children, and what it is like not having a proper diet, or even not having anything to eat. A young woman, Ndalula, who often came to our house, was suffering from kwashiorkor (severe protein malnutrition). She was perhaps eighteen or twenty years old but looked sixty-five. She was listless, and her hair was white. Ndalula was pregnant, unmarried, and living with her father, an alcoholic. She already had one child who was about eighteen months. Even though I had been giving her some food from time to time, it was obvious she needed more help.

Ken McGill, a Presbyterian missionary doctor, used to fly in every three weeks to see patients at the clinic. During one visit, Ken met Ndalula. He suggested that I give her a scrambled egg, some fruit, and a glass of milk every day, and I would see a dramatic difference. When I asked her to meet me every morning for an egg, fruit, and milk, and to bring her child as well, she exclaimed, "Oh, no, no, no! I cannot do that! If I eat that egg, I will become a man."

"Who told you such a thing?"

"Oh, we know that."

I learned that women were indeed being told not to eat eggs; I suspect by the men who wanted eggs for themselves. I reminded her that the doctor had said she needed the eggs and milk, and if she wanted me to help her, that was what she would have to eat. Ndalula asked if I couldn't give her something else. She really wanted manioc, but since it has little nutritive value, I refused. The next day she came up the walkway. "I shouldn't do this, but okay," she said. "I'll eat an egg." She ate the scrambled egg, drank the milk, and gave her child a banana and milk. She came back every day after that until after the birth of her second baby, about two or three months later. As time progressed, I gave Ndalula a half dozen eggs and some bananas to take home, so she was not making daily visits.

I do not know when she began changing. It was so gradual. One day at a women's meeting at church, I saw an energetic young woman with black hair skipping down the path. I asked one of the older women who she was. The woman laughed, "Oh, that's your daughter!" (In African tradition, once you help someone, it is as if you are taking them into your family.)

By the summer of 1969 when we were getting ready to go back to the U.S. for our furlough, Ndalula was coming to church with her two children and seemed to have her life in order. However, her dad was still drinking heavily, and it was rumored he had even used his daughter as a prostitute in the community at one time. Several days before we were to leave, we noticed a man coming up our walkway with Ndalula. I realized it was her father.

"What are you going to do about my daughter?" he asked.

"What do you mean? She looks great and the children seem healthy."

"Yes, but you helped her and she's yours now."

At that I became quite angry: "Sir, you're her father. I understand you drink a lot. I believe if you would straighten yourself up and assume your responsibility, this young lady and her two children would be happy, and the money you spend on drinking could be used for food for them. She is your daughter. The Lord gave her to you and expects you to take care of her. We also hope you will go to church with your daughter and grandchildren. We are asking Pastor Kandau to keep an eye out for her and her children." After leaving on furlough in 1969, we never returned to Moma. However, we felt confident that Pastor Kandau and his wife would help Ndalula and her family in the weeks and months ahead.

We came to the U.S. for a year's furlough from June 1969 to June 1970. Bill worked at the Board of World Missions in Nashville as a missionary-in-residence. It was a difficult year for me physically. I had pneumonia four times and problems with asthma and allergies. Guv Pennington was my doctor during this time and took wonderful care of me. He was a Presbyterian elder and we became good friends. During one of my check-ups, a nodule was found in my neck. I ended up having several tests and saw thirteen doctors during that period. None of them thought the growth in my neck was cancerous, but it was decided that I needed to have the nodule removed. A friend had given me a book to read the night before my surgery by an Episcopal lay leader, Ann White, who was involved in healing ministries. As I leafed through her book that night, I read about her son who had had asthma and that a malignant nodule was discovered and removed from his thyroid gland. I think the Lord meant for me to read this, because for the first time I began to consider the possibility that my nodule might be malignant.

After the surgery, the surgeon told Bill that the operation had been longer than he expected, and the nodule was harder than he had anticipated. Early one morning three days later, Dr. McCloud came into my hospital room and told me the nodule was malignant. The first thing I said in a raspy voice was, "Can I go back to Africa?" He answered, "I certainly hope so." The doctors decided I did not need chemotherapy. The nodule had been wound around one of my vocal cords so the surgeon had to strip much of it off. However, he did not remove the entire nodule because if he had done that, I would not have had a voice. The surgeon did remove one vocal cord. We have joked since then that I do pretty well without it! But at the time the doctors weren't sure what the prognosis was. I was glad they decided I did not need to have chemotherapy, but I was given some pretty strong doses of Synthroid and other thyroid medicines. I remember my life was difficult for a couple of months because I was trying different medicines. Some of the newer synthetic thyroid medicines just did not work for me, so I went back to taking Synthroid. Gov Pennington told me jokingly when Bill and I were about to go back to Congo, "Nancy, you can just go out and find a thyroid gland of a pig, dry it, and eat it!" I told him, "Thanks a lot! I'll remember that. I doubt I'll do it, though!" Guv later came to visit us in Zambia and Zimbabwe and got to see Presbyterian work first-hand.

Bill and I were due to return to Congo that summer; however, I was still quite weak from the surgery. In May, when I went to Orlando to visit Mother and rest, I heard that Ann White was in town. I told Mother and my sister Peggy that I wanted to go to one of her healing services. They agreed to go with me. That evening we sat in the back of the church where she was speaking. Ann invited anyone who would like prayers for healing to come to the front of the church. She had a prayer for me and for each one who came forward. Her hand felt very warm on my head. She told me, "I have a message for you that I'd like to give you if you'll come back tomorrow." I told her I would come. The next day she told me that while she was praying for me the night before at the front of the church, God gave her the passage in Luke 17:11–19 where the ten lepers came to Jesus to be healed. He told them to go and present themselves to the priests. And the scripture says, *as they went along their way, they were healed*. Healing was not immediate, but all were healed as they went about doing what they were told to do. (Only one came back to thank Jesus.) I learned that healing is a process that does not always happen at once. But *as we go on our way, doing what Jesus tells us,* we often reap the benefits. I felt this was an assurance from God that I was in his hands, and I understood it to mean that God was saying I should go back to Congo. It was to be a step in faith, but that's what faith is all about: giving hope. Hebrews 11:1 says, "Now faith is being sure of what we hope for and certain of what we do not see." I thanked Ann and told her what her book had meant to me when I was in the hospital before I had my surgery.

A New Congo Assignment

In July 1970 we returned to Congo for three more years. Unlike the calm years during our first term, these years were chaotic. Bill was appointed field secretary to serve as a liaison between the Presbyterian Church in the U.S. and the Presbyterian Church in the Congo. We lived the first year in Mbuji Mayi, the diamond capital of the West Kasai region. Our house was a large duplex made available for missionary housing by MIBA, the Belgian diamond mining company. Our home served as a guesthouse for visiting missionaries, other visitors and friends, and even the U.S. ambassador. I home-schooled both children, Elizabeth in third grade and William in first.

That year William nearly died of malaria. He had a fever of 105. We called a Belgian doctor to come to our house in the middle of the night. He sat with our son and said if William made it through the night, he would be okay. As you can imagine, there was a lot of praying in our family that night. When the fever broke, we felt God's protection yet another time.

In Mbuji Mayi we had our first experience with a pet monkey. Tiny, a mustached quenon, stayed in a tree with a little belt around its waist, but every now and then he would get loose and terrorize everyone. If we were eating, he tried to grab our food. Merle Baker, a young volunteer from the Mennonite church, was a particular target. He smoked. Tiny often reached into his pockets to grab his cigarettes and matches. Our children enjoyed playing with Tiny and still love to recount the tales of Tiny's escapades.

A wonderful event during this term was that our third child, Shamba, was born. It was a difficult pregnancy. At two months I became very sick, and in March 1971 I had to leave Mbuji Mayi with the children to come back to the States. Thankfully, I stayed with my mother in Orlando, and Elizabeth and William went to Audubon

Park Elementary School in her neighborhood. Bill joined us in June. We made the decision that I would go back to Congo for Shamba's birth. Several doctors in Orlando thought that this decision was strange, even amusing. As it turned out, it was an unusual birth.

When we returned to Congo in August 1971, we moved to Lubondai in the East Kasai region where Central School, the mission boarding school that covered fourth through eighth grades, was located. My mother came to Congo with us and taught another year at Central School. Elizabeth attended fourth grade there while Mother and I taught William, now a second grader, at home.

As my pregnancy progressed, I got quite large, and Bill was worried because there were no doctors nearby. There was a nurse on the station, but he often got drunk after work. Bill would have nightmares and wake up in a cold sweat thinking, "Nancy's in labor; where should I go and what should I do?" Walt Hull, a missionary doctor in obstetrics and gynecology, was a close friend. Walt recommended that I fly to Bibanga, the mission station where he worked in a hospital with a missionary nurse and Congolese staff. So six weeks before Shamba was born, they flew me to Bibanga and I stayed with Virginia King, a wonderful missionary nurse and a dear, precious friend. Her late husband, Earl King, had died suddenly only a few months earlier. He had been field secretary for Congo, responsible for all 162 Presbyterian missionary personnel, and Bill had been chosen as his successor. Virginia took excellent care of me, even as she grieved the loss of her husband.

The day I began to feel labor pains I walked over to Walt and Nancy Hull's home and announced that I was in labor. The Bibanga hospital was about a half mile away—not a hard walk unless you're in labor. Walt was going to drive me in the mission Land Rover, but when he tried to start it the car wouldn't go. He said, "Nancy, even though you're having labor pains, we're going to have to walk," and added jokingly that I should get with it because African women do this all the time. I knew he was trying to get my mind off my labor pains. I had packed my little suitcase with my asthma medicines and a change of clothes. Walt carried the suitcase as we walked to the hospital. What a picture we must have made: the doctor with the *very* pregnant little missionary lady. When we arrived, he hoisted me onto a gurney. The labor pains were coming pretty quickly. As I was being wheeled down the walkway to the operating room, they chased goats away and probably some chickens. Now, as I think back, I wouldn't take anything for that experience, for you certainly wouldn't have chickens and goats running around a hospital in the U.S.!

Because of the difficult pregnancy, I had decided to have a tubal ligation. A young Congolese male nurse said to Dr. Hull, "Why are you doing a tubal ligation on this woman? She's still young (I was thirty-three) and could have a lot more children!" Walt said quickly, "Well, her husband has signed the papers!" In Congo, the wife could not have anything done unless the husband had agreed and signed for it. In fact, Walt did not have a signed note and told me to nod my head to show that I knew what was happening and wanted it done. So I nodded my head. But later we laughed and laughed about what that nurse said, because in the African tradition he thought I should have had at least three more children.

Birch Rambo, another special missionary doctor and good friend, came to Bibanga to be present for the birth. There was a policy that whenever missionaries or their family members were operated on, a second expat doctor would be present if possible, since missionary wives and children had died in the past. When I first told Walt I was in labor, he had immediately called on the CB radio. There was one seat on the plane coming that day and they said they could put either Bill in it, or Dr. Rambo. Bill gave up the seat, since he knew Birch would be of much more assistance in the delivery room.

A short time after Shamba was born, I was taken back to Virginia King's house. She looked after me lovingly and took wonderful care of Shamba. We named the baby for Shamba Samuel, a Presbyterian pastor, head of the Department of Evangelism for the Presbyterian Church of Congo, who traveled a lot with Bill. I stayed four or five days before flying back to Lubondai to be with Bill, my mother, Elizabeth and William. Within two months, however, we found ourselves back in Bibanga for Elizabeth to have her appendix out. She kept it in a jar for many years.

During that year at Lubondai we helped close and pack up Central School, which had been the school for missionary children for many years. We were moving the school to Kananga, the capital city of East Kasai region, because there were not enough missionary students at Lubondai to keep the school going. When Central School was closed in June 1972, PCUS gave the buildings to the local Presbyterian community who continued to use them for a school.

We were so pleased that Pastor Shamba Samuel was able to visit us while we were still at Lubondai and assist in baptizing our son Shamba, his namesake. The Sunday that Shamba was baptized, Bill was asked to assist with the other baptisms also, thirty-six babies and small children. Thirty-five were Zairian and our son was the only *mutoka* (Tshiluba for "white one"). Bill wasn't given all of the children's names until the time for their baptism. Luckily, he had a pen and wrote the names on the palm of his hand. My mother was present, along with Elizabeth and William and others from Central School and the surrounding community. What a joyful and unforgettable experience this was!

Another time we really felt God's presence occurred when Bill took a pastor and his wife to some Presbytery meetings in our Land Rover. Being the youngest evangelistic missionary, Bill had been given one of the oldest Land Rovers. On this occasion, Bill had to travel over some extremely bad roads. Somehow, I had had an anxious feeling—a nudge from God I call it—and I was really praying about this trip, even before Bill left. He was to have arrived at Bob and Mary Gould's home in Mbuji Mayi in time to spend the night. The Goulds were Presbyterian missionaries and very close friends, and I was thankful we had radio contact with them. When evening came, even though he'd left early in the morning, Bill had not arrived. We all were concerned; perhaps he'd had a wreck. I remember clearly that I did not have a sense of fear, but I do remember praying when I learned that Bill had not arrived. That night I was able to sleep because I felt God's peace.

Bob was going to the same meeting as Bill and offered to backtrack on the road where Bill would have driven. By the time Bob found Bill and the car, it had been over 24 hours that Bill had been missing. Bill had come to a huge washout in the road. He was going only about fifteen m.p.h., but he couldn't see the washout ahead. In God's mercy, the car didn't roll over and no one was hurt, but the car was badly damaged and could not be driven. When the accident occurred, the pastor's wife was thrown up toward the roof of the car and yelled, "We've been killed!" Thanks be to God that was not true! When Bob found them, he towed the car, and they went into town to attend the meeting, leaving the car to be worked on. It took quite a while for the Land Rover to be fixed. Again, I remember thanking the Lord for Bill's safety. Later we found out that Bill and I were on the prayer list for that very day in *These Days*, the Presbyterian devotional book used across the Presbyterian Church (US). So, the Lord had people praying for us even before the wreck occurred. That was quite a powerful experience for us—to know that we were in the will of God, and Bill was in His arms of protection.

During this time, we were seeing more and more that life had become extremely hard for our sisters and brothers in the Democratic Republic of the Congo because of the policies of President Mobutu, who had come into power in 1965. Mobutu had people killed if they disagreed with him. During the year we lived in Mbuji Mayi we would hear tales of his taking diamonds for his personal use. Shortly thereafter, he was listed as one of the wealthiest men in the world. The beauty and the riches of Congo are well known; the people of this land should not have had to work so hard just to get by. The wealth that rightfully belonged to the people was used instead to fund Mobutu's opulent lifestyle. It was illegal for average people to have diamonds in their possession, and the Congolese were frequently searched at airports in an attempt to find diamonds stashed somewhere.

On one occasion Bill and I were traveling with Pastor Mbiya, who was the legal representative for the Presbyterian Church in Congo (CPZ). Somehow the men had gone through the line first, but I was stopped by airport security. Almost before I knew it, the women officials motioned for me to come with them. I found myself in a room with two policewomen who wanted a bribe. They had laid out on the counter rubber gloves and utensils for probing. I knew what that meant. They told me I would have to give them something or else take off all my clothes and allow them to strip search me. I knew when this happens, they search all the body cavities, and I broke out in a cold sweat. I thought, "This is not what I bargained for when I agreed to come to Africa!" Bill and Pastor Mbiya had gone on through customs and were about to get on the plane as I began yelling for them. The women told me I would not be allowed to board the plane unless I let them search me. I told them I'd just go back home; I didn't need to get on the plane. They kept telling me I needed to give them something and it needed to be something really big. I kept yelling to get out. I guess I'd been in the room for about ten or fifteen minutes when Pastor Mbiya, who is about six-feet, four-inches tall, realized I wasn't with them and turned around. He heard me screaming and burst through the door and let those ladies have it verbally. He took me by the arm and ushered me out of the room and onto the plane. I certainly felt at that point that I owed my life to him. I heard that doctors and dentists who came out to our area were searched at the airport to see if they had diamonds hidden in their body cavities. Apparently, the searches didn't bother some of these men, but it certainly would have bothered me!

Another airport experience I remember was the time Bill and I were leaving on an Air Congo plane that had been overbooked. People rushed the plane. As the stairs were being rolled away from the plane, people were still standing on them and beating on the side of the plane, trying to get in. Overbooking happened often, and frequently the last seats on the plane were given to whoever would pay the highest price.

In 1967, university students in Kinshasa spoke out and openly rioted against Mobutu and his repressive policies, because they didn't have food, books, or other necessities. In a ruthless act of retaliation, Mobutu sent troops to kill these students. After shooting about two hundred fifty students in cold blood, the soldiers dug a big trench and buried their bodies. Mobutu denied the story on international news, and sadly the U.S. ambassador chose to accept his word. But in Kasai Province, we talked to parents of some missing students who were convinced that these events had happened, because their children never came home. We frequently heard stories like this one, but the U.S. was pretty much rubber-stamping whatever Mobutu said and did. By the early 1970s, the U.S. was beginning to give Mobutu military aid, so that he had a well-trained army to do his bidding. Sadly, whenever he wanted someone tortured or killed, these soldiers carried out his wishes.

Congo was renamed Zaire on October 27, 1971. Mobutu changed the name of the country, the river, and the money to what he called "the three Zs." These years were certainly not easy for the Zairians, especially the women. They went to the fields with their children and worked to raise *tshiombe* (manioc) so that they could cook bedia for their family. They also raised corn and some vegetables, all this using a short-handled hoe to work the soil. It was backbreaking work to eke out a meager existence.

In spite of the hard times, people were coming to Jesus and the churches were beginning to be full. Many of the African pastors we knew were eloquent. Not all had a formal education, but they spent a great deal of time reading the Word, memorizing it, and laboring over their messages. Often their messages were forty-five to fifty minutes long, and the worship services lasted two hours or more. The services were certainly lively, with drums and many choirs. We enjoyed dancing up the aisle with others in the congregation to present our offering. We always had a sense that God was present in these services and that God was being honored. Sometimes now it is hard for us to worship in the quiet, orderly church services here in the U.S.

We saw that our friends, our brothers and sisters in Christ, were not having an easy time, and some of them were afraid to speak openly against Mobutu because of the control he had. There were few paved roads in the country and a very poor communication system, which suited Mobutu. Kananga, with a population of about a half million, was called the largest unelectrified city in the world.

Mobutu did not like the Baluba people from the Kasai provinces, mainly because they were critical of his leadership and spoke openly against him. There were some Baluba who managed to come into positions of important leadership, and Mobutu had several of them killed. One method to rid himself of an opponent was to throw a big celebration for him. As the honored guest was leaving, Mobutu would have him followed and killed. The president did this more than once.

In June 1972, our family moved to Kananga where Bill continued to serve as field secretary and I taught missionary children, including our own. Shamba was then eight months old and already walking. Elizabeth was a great help with him. When we had closed the school at Lubondai, there was a local chief near the village who demanded a lot of Central School's books, materials, and furnishings. We didn't want a fight with him, so we gave him what he wanted. We sorted through the books and materials and took what would be needed for the new school that I was to start in Kananga. For the move, we had packed things in missionary barrels (55-gallon metal drums) and loaded them on a truck. We found a house for our family to rent, and another house nearby for the new school.

Shortly after we arrived, the PCUS mission board in Atlanta called Bill back to the States for fifty days. I felt like I had been dumped in Kananga, left behind in the new house with the children and all our belongings. Thankfully, I did have a wonderful Congolese lady Mama Luta who moved with us to help with Shamba. During those fifty days we had no electricity. The water came on only from 1:00 to 3:00 am in the morning. There were "missionary barrels" on the roof of the house we rented. The spigots had to be turned on so the water would fill the barrels, but then they had to be turned off as soon as the barrels were full, or the water would overflow onto the roof. I remember vividly that before I went to bed, I had to be sure that the spigots were open. The sound of the water coming on in the middle of the night woke me up, and as soon as the barrels were full, I would run out and turn the spigots off. There was never a dull moment!

I was so glad Bill had taught me how to light a Coleman lantern, because that was the only light we had at night. Thankfully, Elizabeth was always there to help, and she liked to cook. She was in fifth grade by then, and William was in third. He liked to ride his bike and play with the neighbor boys. Shamba wasn't any help, but he brought joy to everyone. He was always so outgoing, greeting visitors with great exuberance. Children from all around us would call to him when passing our house and Shamba would run out to the porch and wave.

Some interesting pets joined our family that year in Kananga. We were given a baby monkey, our second mustached quenon. The monkey stayed in a mango tree in our back yard. He had a little belt around his waist and a long rope that allowed him to get high up in the tree. Being clever, he would chew through the rope periodically. He loved to come into the house and get into mischief. Once he jumped on the table while we were eating and grabbed Jello with his hands. It was comical to watch him try and eat it as it slipped through his fingers.

In front of our house there was an area that had once contained a fountain, but the fountain had broken and only a deep pit remained. Dr. Johnny Miller, who loved crocodiles as well as snakes, asked if he could put some crocodiles in the pit. I thought he was joking and agreed, but one weekend he came by with three crocodiles in bags and dumped them in the fountain. The children were fascinated with their new "pets." We had to put a safety fence around the pit eventually because the Zairian kids, many of whom had never seen a crocodile, would come by to look at them. I would trade them an old *Time* magazine for a live frog to feed to the crocs. The Zairian children would not actually touch the frogs because young boys believed your sex would change if a frog spit on you. Instead, the boys would bring the frogs in on a string, and we would drop them into the pit for the crocodiles to eat.

One time I asked a group of boys how they knew about these crocs. "Well, on Sunday we have a routine," they explained. "We go to Mass, and then we come over to see the crocodiles." The Catholic church was located just around the corner from our house. We had these reptiles for about eight or nine months. Eventually, the pit got dirty and Bill had to crawl in to clean it. He put on boots and worked on one end while I tried to distract the crocodiles at the other end. Quite a circus act! When we got ready to leave Kananga, the Presbyterian missionary couple moving into the house did not appreciate the crocodiles. They insisted that Johnny come to remove them before they would live in the house.

That summer of 1972 with Bill gone was not easy. One problem was the head of the Presbyterian Church in Zaire: he drank too much. He would come to our home on many evenings, already drunk. He wanted to talk with me about various subjects. How I wished for Bill! I would dread seeing this pastor come because I didn't have the time to spare and talking with him when he was drunk was impossible. I must admit, though, it did supply some comic relief at times, and the Lord allowed me to laugh in the midst of it.

The pastor had a car that he'd often have to push to get started. He would arrive at our house, pushing the car into the driveway. Then he would start calling people to help him. That meant he'd be with us an hour or two while he'd wait for someone to come and help him start the car. I got to the point where I'd just offer him something to eat and then go take care of the kids. I remember thinking, "Bill, you're in America with running water and electricity, enjoying yourself with all the niceties, while I'm out here with all of this!" We heard that the pastor did give up drinking later and returned to fruitful ministry and even went to England.

God sustained us and gave me the ability to endure and persevere (Romans 8). Now I can look back and see how God was teaching me patience. In spite of my frustrations, I realized I was where God wanted me to be.

Helping to start the new school in Kananga was not easy. We had a Mennonite missionary friend, Marge Neunschwander, whose two sons were exactly the ages of Elizabeth and William. She agreed to be one of the teachers. In addition, there was a Mission Aviation

Fellowship couple, Marvin and Evie Bowers, assigned to Kananga. Their two daughters were also the same ages as William and Elizabeth. Evie became the third teacher. We started the school with those six students plus one other. Evie agreed to teach math, but she had to keep in contact with her husband on the radio when he was flying, so the children would leave the house we had rented for the school and go to her house for math. Riding their bikes to their math lessons and back was their recess. Sometimes, of course, they piddled around and lost time.

Later, a wonderful couple came from the States. They were retired elementary school teachers in their seventies, and we were all thrilled when they showed up in Kananga. Situations often happen on the mission field, where God provides just what is needed. We invited them to help, and they decided they would stay and teach in the school. The kids loved them! The man was an artist with beautiful cursive writing. He made elaborate designs on the blackboard. This couple was especially effective with the students because they weren't their parents, more like special grandparents. It can be a struggle to pull back and set up a pupil/teacher relationship with your own child. This couple was creative and loving but, unfortunately, they were with us only about six weeks. They had planned to spend several months until an incident occurred downtown. Even though they were healthy and walked everywhere, they had gray hair and appeared frail. Some Zairian teenagers backed them into a corner and beat them up. We were so thankful that they weren't seriously hurt, but they left soon after that. We couldn't blame them, but the children really missed them, and so did we!

Lamar Williamson and his wife, Ruth Mary, were serving as Presbyterian missionaries in Zaire at this time. Martha, their daughter, had graduated from William and Mary College and had come to Zaire. She wanted to do something helpful and agreed to teach, but we had nowhere for her to stay. Our house had four bedrooms so that each of our children had his or her own room. Elizabeth came in one night and told me, "Mother, I would be glad to move in with Shamba and give Martha my room." At first I thought, "Gee, another person in our house!" But then I realized that if Elizabeth was willing to give up her bedroom and move in with her baby brother, she really wanted Martha to come. We thoroughly enjoyed having Martha work at the school and live with us for six months. Martha was an artist and the children responded well to her. She brought freshness and creativity to our school.

By that time, Bill had come back from the U.S. and we were reunited as a family. There were multiple crises in the country, especially in Kinshasa, the capital city. Some problems occurred at the Methodist-Presbyterian Youth Hostel where Presbyterian children lived while attending TASOK, The American School of Kinshasa. Bill had to mediate and resolve some of these situations, so he ended up traveling a lot that year.

God's hand of protection over our children continued in Kananga. One situation started with the children's love of animals. Elizabeth and William were playing with some elephant shrews when Elizabeth was bitten. An elephant shrew looks like a mouse, small with a long nose. We could not find the shrew to capture it and watch to see if it developed rabies, so Johnny Miller told us Elizabeth would have to have a series of fourteen rabies shots. At that time, the shots were given in the stomach and were quite painful, but she was very brave. We were grateful when she finished the series and did not develop rabies.

In Kananga there were some beautiful places to picnic along the Lulua River. During that year we'd often go to the medical mission station at Tshikaji, about seven miles away, where we'd play games and have fellowship. Bill enjoyed playing tennis with Ralph Shannon, Walt Hull, Marge Hoffeld, and others. We would take food and go almost every Saturday that we were free. It was a short distance to Tshikaji, but the roads were terrible, so it could take us half an hour or more to get there. Often the military would put up roadblocks that would add fifteen minutes or more to our travel time. The military had the right to stop people, usually hoping a bribe would be paid. For these occasions we had Bibles that we gave out. Some called them missionary bribes. Roadblocks were especially prevalent when there were political problems, and you never knew when violence might break out. Many times the soldiers had been drinking and were unruly.

Zairian police and military were known throughout Africa to be corrupt and undisciplined. We had many encounters with them over the years. I used to joke that I could write a book entitled *Police I Have Encountered and Run From*. They would do anything they could to stop you for minor infractions in order to ask for a bribe. For example, in Kananga there were several one-way streets that were not marked. Signs had been present many years before, but they had faded and weren't visible anymore. My mother was in the car one day when I was driving with Elizabeth and William. I went up a street the wrong way, and a policeman stepped out and stopped me. He said I was going the wrong way. I asked him to show me the sign. He said, "Madam, the sign is not there now but it *was* there, and everyone knows this is a one-way street." He directed me to drive to a certain spot. There, the policeman looked up at someone standing on a balcony, evidently the place where his superior officer was standing. The superior was apparently the one who would decide what the cost would be for me to bribe my way out of this situation.

Mother, coming from the U.S., was telling the children, "Now the police are our friends and there won't be a problem." Elizabeth said, "But Grandmother, he wants to arrest Mother!" Mother said, "Oh no, Elizabeth, that won't happen." "Yes, Grandmother, he keeps saying he's going to take Mother off." Elizabeth and William both spoke Tshiluba, so they understood what the policeman was saying. We were there about an hour, and I'm sure I gave out Bibles to those who detained us. I may even have had to give a money bribe, although we tried hard not to do that. We saw these police and military so often that if we started giving bribes, we would have to continue it. A lot of the businesspeople constantly paid bribes in cash. We handed out copies of the four Gospels, the New Testament, and Bibles.

Another time I was stopped at a circle where two streets came together in the center of Kananga. The circle had been painted at one time. The car entering the circle on the right had the right-of-way. That day when I was driving, one of my tires apparently had touched the invisible circle. The policeman stepped out and stopped me. I knew exactly what was about to happen, but I just smiled. You never wanted to look like you were rattled. He asked me to get out of the car and show him my driver's license. I did this and we talked a bit. He looked at my license and looked up in surprise. He said, "Madam, you were born on November 15. I was too! That makes us practically family. I'll need to let you go. I just can't fine someone who was born on my birthday." I thanked him and drove on. It was a game of wits and luck.

Another time, a missionary friend of ours was in a hurry. Her husband was a dentist. She was stopped by a policeman and told she was speeding. This was ridiculous because no one could speed on those bad roads. He said, "I'll have to take you to jail." She told him, "Oh no, I can't go with you because I have to get dinner ready for my husband, the dentist. He'll be very upset with me if I'm not home to fix his dinner." So, he let her go! Again, it was just a game of cat and mouse.

Second Furlough
and Chattanooga

In the summer of 1973, we were due for a furlough. Bill had gotten sick in the spring, and the doctors were not quite sure what his illness was. Stress could have been part of the problem; our days were full, full, full. When we left, we knew another missionary family would probably be moving into our rental house, and I regret that I did not have time to clean out all the dressers before our departure. Missionary friends came to help as we were packing up. "If you see anything you think I might want," I told them, "save it for me and I'll get it at the end of the year. Just dump everything else."

We spent our furlough year at Mission Haven in Decatur, Georgia. Elizabeth and William walked to Winona Park Elementary School where Elizabeth was in sixth grade and William in fourth. Bill served as a missionary-in-residence at the PCUS headquarters in Atlanta, and we spoke in many churches. I kept busy caring for Shamba and the family, as well as interacting with students at Columbia Seminary. We appreciated being close to Bill's father, Lucian, as well as Bill's brother, Frank, his wife, Mary Ann, and their children.

Bill and I prayed about whether to return to Zaire after our furlough. Elizabeth would have to go to school fifteen hundred miles away in Kinshasa, and we didn't feel ready for that. In two years, we'd be facing the same problem with William. By the time we left Kananga, Bill had had three years of being field secretary and was not sure he wanted to continue in that job. Being head of missionary personnel and chief problem solver with partner churches in Zaire had been a heavy responsibility. As we prayed, the Lord confirmed that we should not go back to Zaire at that time.

A year later in June, Bill received a call from the Presbytery of

East Tennessee, and we moved to Chattanooga to start a new con-gregation that became New Hope Presbyterian Church. Bill was born in Chattanooga and grew up there. His mother, Martha, and sister, Barbara, lived in that area along with other extended family members. It was another period in our lives where we didn't have to move, and we had a wonderful congregation. We were pleased to be present for Barbara's wedding to Richard Brown on May 3rd, 1975.

The Presbytery of East Tennessee had bought a house in Chat-tanooga for the manse. We moved in during the summer of 1974 and held church in our garage. We set up chairs in the garage and brought in a piano. Small kids were cared for in the house. Soon the new church was meeting there every Sunday. By the time we had forty to forty-five people attending, we were organized and bought property at 7301 Shallowford Road. On Easter Sunday 1975, the church had its first service in the house on the property. We began building a sanctuary and multi-purpose building in 1978 and the dedication was held April 22, 1979. Our ten years with the mem-bers of New Hope Presbyterian church were special, and we formed many deep friendships.

When Pastor Tshimunga Mayela, secretary-general of the Pres-byterian Church in Kinshasa, came to visit us, Bill was serving as chairman of our subdivision's homeowners association. Since there were no African-Americans living in our neighborhood, Bill alert-ed the homeowners association that we were going to have a visit from an African pastor. That was fine with the council; Pastor Tshi-munga was from Africa and was no threat (that is, he would not be trying to move in). Pastor Tshimunga stayed with us for several days and liked to go out for walks. He told us that everyone was quite friendly. He was greeted with smiles and "So you're from Africa!" He added, "I don't know how they knew that." We did not tell him.

Later we had another visitor, our friend Bernie Smith, an Afri-can-American pastor living in Canada. Bernie had an incredible voice and had led the singing for many years at the Urbana Mission Conference in Illinois. When Bernie came to visit, Bill hadn't said anything ahead of time to the homeowners association. Every time Bernie went out to walk, neighbors smiled and greeted him with, "We know you're from Africa." One day someone came to visit us. Bernie opened the door and they said, "Oh, you must be working for the Warlicks." These incidents reminded us that things were not all right in our country. We had hoped to see our sub-division become integrated, but it didn't happen while were there.

I taught Bible at East Lake Junior High School in downtown Chattanooga for seven years. It was a privilege to be part of the Bible in the Public Schools program, a project begun by several bankers in Chattanooga in the 1970s. I was glad to be assigned to East Lake, because it was integrated, about half white and half African-American. The students had to have written permission from a parent to be in my class. Each year almost the entire student body took the optional Bible course that I taught. Along with the daily lessons, I was able to show a series of excellent movies filmed in Israel, one series on the book of Genesis (from the Genesis Project), the other the *Jesus Film,* about Jesus as told in the Gospel of Luke. (The *Jesus Film,* a Campus Crusade project, is now the most widely distributed film in history, translated into 1,600 languages and seen by billions worldwide.)

During Bernie Smith's visit, I received permission from the principal for him to speak to my Bible class. The students were happy to hear from him, particularly the African American students. We had our Bible lesson and then Bernie said, "You may ask me anything you want to." One of the African American boys stood up and said, "I'd like to ask you if you beat your wife." I was shocked, but Bernie was so good with his answer: "You know, I could beat my wife. I'm stronger than she is. But no, I don't, because I love her, and I want to cherish her and protect her." That was such a teachable moment for that young man and for the other students. Bernie fielded many more questions. It was a precious time of opening up to someone they trusted, but also of talking about the Gospel in what I like to call "a real-life setting."

Many of the students in my class had tough lives—maybe not as hard as the lives of children I taught in Africa, but certainly life in inner-city Chattanooga was no picnic. Too many of these children didn't seem to have a caring adult in their lives. I'd often see them in the morning at a nearby grocery store drinking a Coke and eating a candy bar before class. No wonder they had trouble sitting still! I enjoyed those seven years at East Lake Junior High and was pleased that I got to know many of my students well. Each day was a learning experience for me, almost like being in a different culture. On Fridays, I always tried to do something special with my class. When I asked what they would like to do, most often my students wanted to hear about Africa. They liked hearing stories and seeing photos of African people, especially the youth. There was one young African American girl in class whose family was very poor. Her clothes were always disheveled, and her tennis shoes had holes in them. She came up to me one day and gave me a dollar. "I'd like for you to send this to the kids in Africa." Was this her lunch money? At first, I wasn't going to accept it, but then I realized I mustn't deny her the opportunity of giving. I was very touched by her generosity. There were other tender moments during those years at East Lake Junior High. It was a privilege to be part of my students' lives. Many of them were amazing, and I was pleased that they liked to hear the Bible stories and responded so positively to what they were studying. I visited some of them at home, which helped me realize just how hard their lives were. I prayed that each one would have a good life.

My work with Bread for the World started during our time in Chattanooga as I was confronted by the poverty and hunger in the inner-city and elsewhere. While prayer is a vital part of our Christian life, God also calls us to act on our convictions and fight for those who have no voice. Bread for the World, an ecumenical Christian advocacy organization started by Reverend Art Simon in 1974, offered me a way to advocate for laws that would improve the lives of so many who go hungry.

During those ten years in Chattanooga, our family enjoyed our African grey parrot. These parrots are incredibly intelligent, sociable, and can mimic all sorts of sounds— even music and conversations. A missionary colleague gave our first parrot to Bill as a small bird. I think its mother had died. To begin with we kept him in a little cage. Our children named him Nyunyu, "bird" in Tshiluba. He was not able to talk or mimic at first, just "chirp, chirp, chirp" for weeks. Bill said, "I think if I hear that bird chirp one more time ...!" But then the parrot began to mimic us, and we grew to love him. Years later we had a screened-in porch in our house in Kinshasa, which we turned into an aviary with tree branches and stands for our two African greys.

We had decided to take Nyunyu back to the States with us in 1973 when we went on furlough. Sabena Airlines agreed to transport the bird unaccompanied on a flight to the U.S. for $100. We sent Nyunyu to my mother in Orlando. Mother reported that someone called one day to see if she was home, and about thirty minutes later a customs official showed up with the parrot. He said, "We've got this parrot for you. We've had it in quarantine, but we don't know what to do with it or what to feed it. We're going to give it to you. But if it dies, you need to call us." He then gave her his card.

Mother kept the parrot for us the year we were in Decatur. Many of our family and friends enjoyed Nyunyu. Mother's mailman said the parrot got him in a great deal of trouble. Whenever he was putting letters in the box and an attractive young lady passed by, the parrot would whistle, and the lady would turn and think the mailman had done it. At that time, my sister Jane and her family lived across the street. The parrot would call their dog, Sophie, in Jane's voice and the dog would come running. It was so funny to see this!

We brought Nyunyu to Chattanooga in 1974 and kept him in the kitchen in a great big cage. He talked, laughed, and learned to whistle the tune from "The Andy Griffith Show." We often let him out to walk around the house. When the doorbell rang the parrot would say "Come in" in Bill's voice or mine. When the phone rang, he would answer "Hello" in my voice and then laugh, "Ha, ha, ha!" The bird loved me and would follow me around. When I wanted to talk on the phone, sometimes he was obnoxious, and I had to shut the door. Nyunyu would then peck on the door until I opened it and let him in. Over the years, we did have a lot of fun with him.

During the first months we were in Chattanooga, when the church was meeting in our house, we told people we had taught the bird to say several phrases, but whenever people were there for Bible study or church services, it was as if the bird was frozen; he wouldn't speak a word. However, one night we were closing a Bible study with a time of prayer, and all at once Nyunyu yelled out, "Praise the Lord! Amen!" Everyone had a good laugh. When Shamba was three or four, he would get ready to go to bed around 7:30 or 8:00 p.m. Nyunyu would say, "Shamba, go to bed, go to sleep." One night, Nyunyu kept repeating it: "Shamba, go to bed, go to sleep. Shamba, go to bed, go to sleep." Finally, Shamba sat up and said, "Nyunyu, I *am* in bed and I am *trying* to go to sleep!" When we had friends over to play cards, the bird would mimic all our voices. We played one game called Nertz. To win you had to yell "Nertz" when you had cards in a certain order. For weeks, the parrot would yell "Nertz, Nertz" in different voices.

African greys are very smart and live a long time. We had Nyunyu for over ten years. We loved this bird! Sadly, he died before we returned to Zaire. Of course, our family had a funeral service for him.

Those ten years in Chattanooga were good years in so many ways. But we never forgot our years in Congo/Zaire, and we were thankful that we had several African visitors during this time. We also kept getting letters from Zairians asking us to come back. I would read the letters and cry.

The Call Back to Africa

By 1983, Bill felt he had pretty well finished what he had been called to do at New Hope Presbyterian Church. We had over 120 members in the congregation and the church building was completed.[i]

One day Bill got a call from John Pritchard, the PCUS Area Secretary for Africa. He wanted to talk about a new opportunity for us to return to Zaire. John spoke about Alex Booth, a wealthy Presbyterian elder on the Board of Trustees of The Outreach Foundation, a very generous man. Alex was giving financial support to help train pastors and evangelists and to build churches and schools in Zaire. The Outreach Foundation (TOF) was formed in 1979 by a group of Presbyterian ministers and elders who wanted the PCUS denomination to do more in the area of evangelism and church growth. Presbyterians working through TOF were exploring new and exciting ways to work with global partners as these partners preached the Gospel and shared the love of Jesus Christ. The African church was growing rapidly. The need for training pastors and constructing places of worship was (and still is) a priority for African church leaders. The leaders also asked for help in building church schools for primary and secondary school children and in strengthening seminary training for new pastors and evangelists.

Alex Booth felt he was not getting adequate reports from Zaire about the work. He wanted someone on the field to oversee the work and write first-hand reports about what was going on. Bill flew to Charleston, West Virginia, to meet him. It was a good meeting, and Alex felt they could work well together. We heard that Alex commented to John Pritchard that he was glad to meet a pastor "who could do something practical." Alex valued working with your hands and getting them dirty when needed. Bill had the advantage of having had a father and grandfather who owned a construction company. He had learned to lay brick while working for them in the summers and even labored as a hod-carrier (carrying water and mortar) during high school.

By the summer of 1984, we were under appointment to return to Zaire. We were assigned to be coordinators for the Project for Evangelism and Church Growth in Africa (PECGA), covering work in Zaire, Ghana, Cameroon and Equatorial Guinea. PECGA called for a quarter-of-a-million dollars and Alex put up more than half the amount. Several congregations helped support this new project, both financially and with prayers. John Pritchard and Rev. Dr. Cliff Kirkpatrick, Director of the Division of International Missions for the denomination, shared a vision for what could be accomplished in Africa. We were very thankful to be asked to return to Zaire and definitely felt called by God to do this.

Initially, Bill returned to Zaire in September 1984 for forty-five days to assess the situation on the ground in Kinshasa, the capital city, and also upcountry in Kananga. I stayed behind at Mission Haven with Shamba, now an eighth grader. Elizabeth, who had just graduated from Duke University, was starting a two-year term in Zaire as a Volunteer in Mission. She lived and worked at Bulape with Presbyterian missionaries Dr. and Mrs. Ken McGill. Later she came to Kinshasa to work with Annette Kriner, a PCUS missionary nurse. William was in his junior year at King College and stayed to finish his studies.

Bill returned to Atlanta after the fact-finding trip and made his report to Alex, John, Cliff, and the TOF board. Then after Christmas, he returned to Kinshasa where we were assigned to live and work. He found a rental house for us on Avenue Cannas in Limeté, near the Njili International airport in Kinshasa. Shamba and I followed in January. We decided to go to Cairo on our way to Kinshasa, because Shamba was eager to see the pyramids, the Valley of Kings, and other sights in Egypt that he had studied about in school. We had a wonderful time visiting museums in Cairo, investigating the pyramids, and then flying to visit the Valley of the Kings. Unfortunately, sandstorms came up while we were in Egypt, and our planned departure was delayed. Sabena Airlines in Cairo assured me that they had sent word to Bill that our flight was delayed, but later we learned that they had not sent a message. Communication wasn't good then, and airline officials were known to make promises they couldn't keep. Planes in Africa quite often do not fly on time, and back then they *certainly* did not. We nicknamed Air Congo/Air Zaire *Air Peut-etre* (translation: "Air Maybe").

When Shamba and I finally landed in Kinshasa, we worried that no one would be at the airport to pick us up. There was no phone service then, so communication was difficult. Many of us called the airport in Kinshasa "La Guerre" (the War Zone) because it was so chaotic—extremely crowded with thieves everywhere. There were no cell phones in those days, and we were without local currency to take a taxi. We knew that tourists and other visitors could be arrested for trying to pay in U.S. dollars. As it turned out, Bill had come to meet the plane just in case we were on it. Bless him! We were glad to finally get to our new home in Limeté.

Our days were busy that first year. In our newsletter dated March 25, 1986, we wrote:

Let us share a few of the accomplishments of the Project of Evangelism and Church Growth in Africa (PECGA) during this past year. These statistics, however, do not reflect the real joy and enthusiasm of the Presbyterian churches in Zaire (CPK and CPZa) and in Ghana (PCG and EPC). They tell only part of the story. God has blessed the results, and to Him be the glory! In 1985 the evangelism project:

- *built or started to build eighteen new churches*

- *bought eighteen pieces of land to begin new churches*

- *provided "matching funds" for four churches to complete their buildings*

- *built walls around three churches to protect the land*

- *bought two manses and repaired two others*

- *put a concrete floor in one church*

- *provided scholarship help for seventy-eight theological students in Zaire and two in the U.S.A.*

- *provided scholarship help for sixty-three Bible school students in Zaire*

- *supported fourteen evangelists working in rural areas*

- *provided the salaries for three professors of Evangelism in Bible schools*

- *did major repairs at the theological school at Ndesha on student and faculty housing*

- *provided books for graduates of Bible Schools*

- *provided books for the libraries of the Bible Schools*

- *It's been an exciting year for us.*

Though we lived in Zaire, we were responsible for coordinating the PECGA projects in Ghana, Cameroon and Equatorial Guinea as well. At the beginning, many of the PECGA projects outside Zaire were in Ghana. Bill made more trips than I did to Ghana's capital city, Accra, and to Kumasi and rural villages. He traveled with pastors from the Presbyterian Church of Ghana (PCG) or the Evangelical Presbyterian Church (EPG). When entering a village, they would sit with the chief and bring greetings, as well as to let the chief know they would be traveling in his village. On one trip, Bill went with an EPG pastor to see a chief in a rather isolated area. In order to reach the chief's village, they had to cross a creek on a narrow log. They were greeted by the chief who listened to them as they shared the Gospel. Because they had made that trip to his remote village, he made Bill an honorary chief. As part of the ceremony, the chief put his gold cap-like hat on Bill's head. Bill thought, "What a nice souvenir!" However, after the photos were taken and the ceremony was over, the chief took the hat back!

We were impressed by the wise and mature leadership of the Presbyterian Church of Ghana (PCG) and the Evangelical Presbyterian Church (EPG). During this time, Bill was fortunate to spend time with a brilliant Presbyterian man of God, the Rev. Professor

Kwame Bediako. Professor Bediako was appointed Director of Ak-rofi-Christaller Institute of Theology, Mission and Culture located in Akropong, Ghana. This institution has had a far-reaching influence on many Christians in Ghana and beyond. We also met two dedicated young Presbyterian pastors, John Azumah and Solomon-Sule-Saa. Both John and Solomon grew up in Muslim families in Northern Ghana. They became Christians when they went south to study in Presbyterian schools of higher education and were both mentored by Dr. Bediako until his sudden death in June 2008. Bill and I keep in touch with John and Solomon as they continue to serve their Lord faithfully. Solomon is doing outstanding work at the Akrofi Christaller Institute; John spent several years teaching at Columbia Theological Seminary in Decatur (where Bill attended). John has since returned to Ghana where he has founded The Sanneh Institute, a center for advanced studies in Christianity and Islam, named in honor of the late Lamin Sanneh who taught at Yale University and who, like John, was a West African who converted from Islam to Christianity. We thank God for the service of each of these scholarly and godly leaders.

We also visited with church leaders in Cameroon during this period but traveled only once to visit church leaders in Equatorial Guinea. The Rev. Henry Awasom was Moderator of the Presbyterian Church of Cameroon (PCC) at that time. Henry was a godly man with a wonderful sense of humor, and we enjoyed traveling with him. On one occasion, Bill and Henry traveled into an isolated area to visit several Presbyterian congregations. It was a three-day walk for them, and they were warmly received by the Christians. The chief in the area appreciated their visit and held a ceremony to name Bill as an honorary chief. This time Bill got to keep the red wool cap, which the chief gave him as a reminder of the memorable journey.

Our first trip upcountry after returning to Zaire was in the summer of 1985. We flew to Kananga, the capital city of East Kasai province, where we had lived before. Upon arrival at the airport, Bill and I had an unusually pleasant airport experience while we were waiting in line to go through customs. We had lived in Kananga for a year but had been away from the area for eleven years. A dear Presbyterian elder who worked at the airport rushed up to us. He said, "Muambe and Mama, you don't need to wait in line." (Muambe is the name for a missionary pastor.) He turned and said to those around us, "These are missionaries; they're here to help us," and he whisked us through customs. We were amazed that even after all those years, this man remembered us, welcomed us back, and thanked us for returning. This was a very special moment for Bill and me, feeling appreciated and being surprised by God. It was a serendipitous experience, much like being welcomed home.

Bill and I lived in Kinshasa, the capital of Zaire, from January 1985 until September 1991 when we were evacuated due to the civilian riots and revolt of the military against President Mobutu. During those years, we were privileged to work with the Zairian Presbyterian Church (CPK) in and around Kinshasa and with the CPZa, as the church was called in the East and West Kasai provinces. Shamba studied at The American School of Kinshasa (TASOK) that was across town from our home. Elizabeth lived with us and worked with Annette Kriner in public health centers in the capital city for a year and a half. While she was with us, we decided we wanted to attend church together and become active members in a local congregation. We chose Kingabue Presbyterian Church, near one of the health centers where Elizabeth worked. Elizabeth wanted to sing in the choir. She had to try out before being chosen as a member of the main choir, one of several choirs in the church. This *a cappella* choir practiced three times a week under the direction of a talented young man. The choir members called him Michael Jackson, because when he directed the music, he moved like young Michael would undoubtedly have done, had he been a choir director. We had many wonderful experiences worshiping with this congregation.

One Sunday when William was visiting, our family sat together on a rickety wooden bench. In the middle of the worship service, the bench broke into two pieces with a very loud crash. The pastor continued the service as if nothing had happened. We couldn't laugh and no one else did either.

On the last Sunday before Elizabeth returned to the States in 1986, the pastor cried at the end of his message and several in the congregation also cried as they said goodbye to her. There was a lot of crying on all sides that day!

As part of our involvement with the Project of Evangelism and Church Growth in Africa (PECGA), we were helping congregations that needed a permanent building for worship or needed a tin roof to complete their building. Helping with construction of schools soon followed. Having been away from Zaire for ten years, we saw that even though the church was growing rapidly, and God was at work in a mighty way, the people's daily lives had not improved. Their suffering was painful to witness. Often, I would sit and cry. No one deserves this kind of life—struggling so hard simply to have something to eat. Women had to walk long distances to get water for their families. Many of the pastors, some of them with large families, would share with us how hard life was for them. We had just come from the U.S. where most of us have plenty … even too much! We ourselves had enjoyed a more prosperous life during our ten years in Chattanooga.

Women carrying heavy loads

I remember crying out to the Lord. While some of our Zairian friends had moved ahead academically, they were still struggling to feed their families and to make ends meet. It was a real shock to see friends living in poverty, with no electricity and no access to clean water or proper sanitation. Yet we were inspired to hear from many of our friends, even in the midst of their daily struggles, that they felt their primary goal in life was to serve the Lord Jesus Christ and share His love. They were dedicated to working so that "His Kingdom might come on earth as in heaven."

Sometimes we worshiped in different congregations when Bill was invited to preach. More often than not, however, we attended worship at the Kingabue Presbyterian Church. Each Sunday, the congregation would take up several offerings: one for the pastor's salary, one to help someone needy in the community (perhaps a widow or a grandmother caring for one or more grandchildren), and another for finishing their building.

Many church buildings were incomplete, some with thatched roofs that allowed rain to fall inside during worship. During Alex Booth's yearly visits, he had become very interested in helping to fund church construction and the training of pastors because he had seen how rapidly the congregations were growing. He also saw many unfinished church structures. The members of these congregations were eager to have their Houses of God completed. Some people would put IOU's in the offering plate. During stewardship campaigns, the men and women in the congregations would challenge each other to give more. The elders would bring in a chalkboard. They would say, "The women have pledged this amount of money." The men would then say, "We can't let them outdo us." They would pledge more. Offering time could be quite lively and might last thirty minutes or so, with dancing and singing. We certainly have never seen this kind of excitement at offering time in the States!

One elder in the Kingabue Presbyterian Church pledged that he would give six sacks of cement. The church was trying to finish the walls so PECGA could help them buy the roofing sheets. This elder invited us to eat with his family one Sunday after church. His wife prepared a lovely chicken dinner, which probably was an extravagance for them. As we entered his house, we saw that it was not finished. There was no back wall, only a curtain. Bill and I were amazed that this man and his wife chose to give six sacks of cement to help complete the House of God rather than finish their own home. It was humbling to witness the extent of their commitment to Jesus Christ.

With Pastor Mampasi and his wife on the day of his ordination in 1991 (in front of their church)

Rev. Dr. William (Bill) Bryant became executive director of The Outreach Foundation in 1994. He and his wife, Bette, are very special friends of ours. We had gotten to know them when Bill Bryant was the senior pastor of First Presbyterian Church in Nashville. They and their church supported us and prayed for us. Bill and Bette made several trips to Kinshasa to visit us, see our work, and meet some of our Zairian sisters and brothers in Christ. Once a year, they brought a group of Presbyterians with them. I vividly remember one visit when I took the Bryants to downtown Kinshasa. I parked and engaged a young Zairian to watch our car, which stood out because it was a red Toyota Land Cruiser. I locked the car and agreed to pay him when we came back if the car was okay. We weren't gone long, but upon our return I realized that one of the tires was flat. I looked around to size up the situation and saw two policemen coming our way. As they got to the car, they offered to change the tire. Unfortunately, the police weren't always dependable and often were found to work with thieves. However, I had no choice since I couldn't change the tire myself. By this time, a small crowd had gathered to see what was going on. I asked Bette to guard my purse and hers. Then I asked Bill to watch the policemen as we handed them the tools for putting on the spare. I don't remember if I had time to ask them to pray, but *I* certainly was praying. When the two policemen finished, they gave all the tools back to Bill. I handed them a tip and a Bible for each one. I heaved a sigh of relief as we drove away and thanked the Lord for his protection. We had had quite an adventure!

In October 1986, we had a special visit from Dr. Jim Hardy and his wife, Peen. They came for six weeks to volunteer at one of the Presbyterian hospitals, the Good Shepherd Hospital at Tshikaji, near Kananga. Peen and Jim were members of First Presbyterian Church of Leesburg, Florida, one of our supporting churches. We so enjoyed getting to know them and have remained close friends. Over the years, we have had several memorable experiences with the Hardys, including a ride on an elephant!

In all, there were twenty-four churches built around Kinshasa from 1984 to 1991 with money from Alex Booth, The Outreach Foundation (TOF), and churches and individuals across the PC(U-SA) denomination. There were also fifteen or more primary and secondary schools being built in the city at that time, with others under construction in the Kasai region. Bill and I would often thank the Lord that the resources made available by PC(USA) and TOF allowed our brothers and sisters in Africa to worship in completed churches, although none of the churches were plush by any means. Many had only dirt floors and no electricity. As soon as the church members got a roof on the building, they wanted cement for the flooring. Most of the windows didn't have glass and there was often no door to lock. Consequently, many of the people carried the chairs and benches home with them each Sunday so the furniture wouldn't be stolen. Even with these inconveniences, the congregations continued to grow.

Our backyard always had a supply of cement, lumber, rebar and roofing sheets, so we were a target for thieves. Minuit ("Midnight" in French), our large black dog, was a pet but also part of our security plan. Everywhere we looked in Kinshasa, we saw high walls with broken glass on top, and many people hired guards at night. We knew we needed to hire a night guard, and it became one of my responsibilities to deal with our night guards or sentries. I worried, because when paying a guard to protect property and keep thieves away, there is always the danger that he might be hurt. Since Bill and I usually paid better wages than most people around us, we had no trouble finding workers, but the downside was that people knew what was in our yard. Some of them wound up stealing from us. One guard was an alcoholic and would sometimes be drunk when he came to the house at night. (This always seemed to happen when Bill was away!) We tried to help him, but sadly he was found dead in a ditch one night. We helped his widow as much as we could. We tried to hire guards from one of the Presbyterian congregations as often as possible, since then we could discuss any problems with our amazing foreman, Badibanga Mukeba, who would contact an elder or a pastor if a situation warranted action.

Badibanga oversaw all the construction projects in Kinshasa for PECGA. He was an elder in his Presbyterian church. He loved Jesus Christ and would start each day by praying with his construction team. Badibanga was an honest and gifted builder whom we trusted with large sums of money to buy materials and pay his workers. We felt confident in his oversight of the building projects and thanked God for him.

In addition to Minuit, we had a menagerie of unusual pets: two African grey parrots and a pet monkey, Nikki. Our son William received Nikki, our third mustached guenon, as a birthday gift when he came for a visit in the summer of 1985. In the beginning, Nikki was small and cute, but he grew quite large in the six years we had him. He had a belt around his waist and a long cord tied to a large mango tree in our back yard. One of our workmen had the duty to see that Nikki did not bite through the cord and get loose. In 1990 when William returned to Kinshasa to teach and be the sports director at TASOK, he and Nikki quickly reestablished their bonds.

Increasingly, Nikki would bite through the rope and jump on someone.[ii] One time a lady was passing our house with a huge bowl of baguettes on her head. The monkey jumped out and landed in the bowl. The lady screamed and ran away. She was not hurt, thankfully, but the baguettes were scattered everywhere. Naturally, I bought all of her bread, and it was expensive! We think Nikki became jealous of anyone who diverted William's attention. When Elizabeth visited us the summer of 1991, Nikki bit her ear and she had to have stitches. Another time a man named Joseph came into the yard when the monkey was loose and Nikki bit him, too. Our wonderful Christian cook, Tata Mata, took Joseph to the hospital. Tata Mata read the Bible to him and eventually Joseph accepted Jesus as his Lord and Savior. When we gave Joseph a Bible in Lingala, he was quite pleased.

Shamba with our pet monkey!

During the last year we were in Kinshasa, Nikki became more and more of a problem. He was very hard to catch if he got loose. He would go on rampages, shaking the garage doors next to the mango tree. He was fearsome. To catch him, I put a Valium in a banana. When Nikki became sleepy enough, a worker put his belt back on.

We had a friend who was an advisor to the zoo in Kinshasa. She told us the monkey was full-grown and just needed a mate. She recommended to William that he talk with Jane Goodall, who had come to speak at TASOK. We were considering taking Nikki to a forest area, but Ms. Goodall said that was not a good idea because he had been around people for so long. She told William that the monkey needed to be put down. The next time he got loose, Bill and I captured him in the garage and gave him a Valium banana. Bill petted his hand to keep him calm while I rushed into town to get a shot that was to be given straight into the monkey's heart. We waited for William to return home from school. He gave Nikki the shot and Nikki died peacefully. It was hard for William, but the monkey had become such a menace, there was no alternative.

We received our most unusual animal as a Christmas gift: a pangolin. A gift often given to royalty, pangolins are known as scaly anteaters and look a bit like a pinecone with legs. This most extraordinary creature is becoming extremely rare. That Christmas morning Bill and Shamba had gone to church, but I was sick and stayed at home in bed. I kept hearing a knock and finally realized whoever was knocking was not going away. I opened the door to find a church member from one of the churches Bill had worked with. He was carrying a big cardboard box with a pangolin inside, a gift for us. It was very smelly, and I didn't want to accept it, but this man had probably walked ten or fifteen miles to bring us this present. In the African tradition, I needed to give him a gift in return. I quickly got some rice and cans of sardines for him to take to his family, and I accepted the pangolin. Minuit went wild! I put the box in the kitchen and went back upstairs to bed. The pangolin began to smell worse. Minuit kept barking and trying to get in. When Bill and Shamba got home, I showed them our gift. The next day our workers were quite interested and kept saying what an honor it was for us to have been given this special present. Evidently pangolin is good meat, although I've never eaten it. We looked up information about pangolins in our books and had an interesting school lesson with Shamba. Minuit kept carrying on and finally we decided to give the animal to one of our workers. Of course, the other workers were very jealous because they hadn't been chosen, but we had only one pangolin.

Living in Kinshasa, we heard more and more about the cruelty of President Mobutu. Increasingly he was perpetrating acts of violence and brutality against the people. There were periods when the Zairians were suffering so much that they would call on the United States to take their president because they said the United States had given him to them. It was illegal at this time to speak openly against Mobutu so we decided to pray in our home with the pastors and church leaders who were frustrated with the repressive government. Bill's office was behind our house. While he was in meetings or working on reports, I would have tea and pray with the pastors, many of whom were young and very disheartened. Our home was a safe place for them to share their feelings about what President Mobutu and his government were doing to their countrymen. Many times they told us stories that made me weep. Some of these stories were hard to believe, but after we were evacuated, I came to realize that most of the stories about the violence and evil deeds of their cruel president were indeed true.

Mobutu's specially trained forces and the opulence in which he lived were often subjects of conversation at our gatherings. Mobutu didn't travel by road; he traveled by helicopter, because he was afraid for his safety. Consequently, he was more and more removed from reality. His paranoia was revealed when he went to the city of Kananga in the Kasai region at the invitation of the governor. In preparation for the visit, the fronts of all the buildings were painted, since that was all that Mobutu would see. He was in a motorcade when a car backfired. Although he was in a bulletproof Mercedes Benz, he thought someone was shooting at him. Immediately he directed his chauffeur take him to a safe house where he stayed for several days. Mobutu didn't come out until he went to the airport to leave. We heard that some people lost their lives over that incident. Whenever anything unpleasant happened to him, someone had to pay; that's how obsessed he was with himself. And he hated the people of the Kasai region, because the Baluba people who lived there stood up to him.

By that time, I was participating in campaigns and advocacy efforts. For several years I had been a member of Bread for the World. It was very apparent to Bread for the World and other groups, such as Amnesty International, that Africa needed America's help, and that Zaire was one of those places where life was especially difficult for the people. As Christians, we felt called to stand with our Zairian brothers and sisters in Christ in their hour of need. But because the CIA in the United States was complicit in putting Mobutu into office, I also felt a responsibility that as an American I should speak out against what my government did. I got to the point of apologizing to the Zairians, saying, "I'm really sorry that my government put Mobutu in and has left him to pillage and rape and do whatever he wants to do." I was writing to U.S. senators and representatives, to former President Jimmy Carter and the Carter Center, to Bread for the World, to Amnesty International, and to others about the problems I saw in Zaire.

In 1988, we got word that Senator Sam Nunn, Chairman of the Armed Services Committee, and Senator David Boren, Chairman of the CIA Committee, were coming to Kinshasa. We had many friends at the U.S. Embassy. I had spoken quite frankly to them, so when these high-ranking members of Congress arrived, one of my friends at the embassy said, "Nancy, there's going to be a big reception at Ambassador William Harrop's residence. I'll get you an invitation if you'll speak to your southern senator about some of these problems." At the reception, the ambassador, knowing I was from the South, took me to the head of the reception line and said, "Senator Nunn, here is a lady from Georgia. You two can speak Georgian." At that time, the ambassador supported President Mobutu, even though there had been clear evidence of that horrific killing of many university students in Lubumbashi, including blood on the walls of buildings. The ambassador had reported that only one student died, in accordance with Mobutu's version of the incident.

After the ambassador left us, I told Senator Nunn where I was from, that my husband had gone to Columbia Seminary in Decatur, and that we were missionaries. "Senator Nunn, military help is not the answer to Zaire's problems," I said. He looked at my nametag and said, "Mrs. Warlick, I believe you're right." I responded, "Senator, I *know* I'm right." Then he stepped out of the receiving line and said, "I'd like to talk with you some time. I'd like to meet with a group of missionaries." The senator asked me if there were any other missionaries from Georgia, and I said there were. A missionary couple from Georgia was working at the Methodist-Presbyterian Hostel, so that's where we decided to meet. I had a French New Testament to give to each of the two senators, who thanked me. I knew Senator Boren was a Baptist, and Senator Nunn was a Methodist. Senator Boren told me, "You're going to make Sam Nunn so happy to be able to meet with some of his constituents from Georgia. We just got back from Kenya, and all these Oklahomans were there. Nobody from Georgia!" Later I was told that the number two official at the embassy complained, "This little lady came in waving Bibles!" I laughed and said, "Well, I guess it's better than Bible *thumping*."

That Sunday at the International Church, we put out the word inviting missionaries to come meet with Senator Nunn. About 50 missionaries came, as well as Kay McHaney, wife of the head of Gulf Oil in Zaire. Our son Shamba and several from his class at TASOK made a long banner welcoming Senator Nunn and proclaiming him "the next president of the U.S." Nunn enjoyed seeing this and meeting the students. He told us that his aunt had been a missionary to China, and he had a great respect for missionaries and for what they do.

I had asked some in the group to share several ways that U.S. money had been spent to help the Zairian people: through USAID funding for vaccination programs, clinics, community health work, help for educational programs, and HIV-AIDS awareness. He said he wanted to hear from us about what was going on, so we explained how the U.S. support for President Mobutu was really hurting our Zairian friends. We found out that Senator Nunn really did not like Mobutu. When he returned to Washington, he got the U.S. Senate to cut Zaire's military budget. I was seen as a problem by some at the U.S. Embassy, because they had to cut a position. However, the U.S. Defense Attaché (a Presbyterian) told me that while some at the embassy were unhappy with the budget cut for Zairian military aid, he was *not* unhappy. He was well aware of how U.S. military aid was being used (or misused), how weapons were being given, and how Mobutu was turning these weapons on his own people. I felt pleased and thankful about all this feedback from people who were in high positions and from word that the defense attaché was glad I had said what I did. All along the way, I had informed the attaché as to what we were doing, and he had given his approval. As a Christian, he said it was good that Senator Nunn wanted to speak to the missionaries, although some embassy staff were unhappy that Nunn would rather be with us than at another embassy function. It was pretty humorous that the senator was brought to our meeting in the ambassador's Mercedes-Benz with a big flag, but his chauffeur didn't know where the Methodist-Presbyterian Hostel was located. We had given them directions, but they must have gotten lost. When they finally arrived, the bodyguards placed themselves around the building and came inside to look around and make sure everything was secure. Nunn laughed and said, "Sorry, but this goes with the job." It was a wonderful meeting. We as Christian missionaries were able to speak to a Christian who was a significant leader in the U.S. Congress and who really wanted to hear what we had to say.

When Bill and I returned to the U.S. in 1989, I was invited to Senator Nunn's office in Washington. Evidently the senator had talked to his top staff person with whom I had been communicating about the growing problems with President Mobutu. He wanted me to brief some of his staff about the situation in Zaire. I thought they would be low-level staff, and that was fine, and I had brought some material for them. When I got to his office, they had arranged a really nice meeting room for us. A gentleman in the room, who was an ambassador somewhere in Africa, was already seated. I said, "Nice to meet you. Maybe I'm in the wrong room." He said, "What are you here for?" I responded, "I'm here about a briefing on Zaire." He said, "I'm here for that, too."

I shared from my heart. I told the gathering how bad the situation was for the Zairian people, that the missionary community of expats and the Zairians all knew that something dire was going to happen, that things were boiling over, and that the situation just couldn't keep going as it was. Severe poverty deepened, yet Mobutu lived in opulence with a huge yacht and a fleet of Mercedes-Benz cars—all things he felt were his "due." He was getting rich on the backs of the very people he was supposed to be protecting and serving. Mobutu was really burdening them, pushing their faces in the dirt, dehumanizing them.

I found out later there were people in the U.S. State Department, both Democrats and Republicans, who realized things weren't right in Zaire. But this period was also during the start of the Bosnian war, so the situation in Zaire took a back seat. Mobutu had been in power for twenty-four years and yet, in all this time, only one person had resigned in protest of U.S. policies in Zaire. Someone told me that several people (nine, as I recall) had resigned from the State Department because they disapproved of the U.S. policy in Bosnia. Obviously, there were not many who cared deeply enough about Zaire to resign in protest. People seemed to care more about their jobs in the State Department than about tending to the business at hand, that is, making sure people were not being oppressed. It's sad that by this time the U.S. had poured out probably a billion dollars in overt aid (and who knows how much covert aid), and yet life was no better for the Zairian men, women and children there. Sadly, democracy and human rights were not considered important for Zairians.

After that visit in the U.S., Bill and I returned to Kinshasa. We were quickly caught up again in the work of helping to build churches and schools, taking building supplies from church to church. As we were storing, buying, and delivering supplies like cement and iron bars, the possibility of theft was an ever-present reality. One day a man in a taxi chased Bill, and Bill could see he had a gun. Bill had just picked up a load of cement; he had a good bit of money, too, and someone must have seen it. Bill was able to weave in and out of the traffic and finally lost the taxi. At one point in the chase, the fellow actually leaned out of the taxi window trying to shoot one of Bill's tires and stop his car. We thanked God for protecting

Bill that day and in the days ahead.

Increasingly in 1990, it became apparent that the country was almost grinding to a halt. It was certainly not an easy time to live in Zaire. People later asked us why we stayed so long in the face of all these problems. We felt we were *called* to build up the kingdom of God, to stay and work side by side with our Zairian sisters and brothers, and to be a symbol of the church worldwide. In John 10:10, Jesus said, "I have come that you may have life and have it more abundantly." We wanted a more abundant life for the people of Zaire. We knew that education was so important for the children. We wanted to see construction of neighborhood schools. Because clean water was such a dire need, funds were used for drilling some wells. We were also able to construct much needed medical clinics. Badibanga and his team continued to build churches so people could come to pray and worship, even if it were raining. These church buildings also served as primary schools and community centers where trainings in life skills took place. Presbyterian women held Bible studies, prayer meetings, literacy and sewing classes, and other events in these buildings. All of these buildings were identified as priorities by the CPK and CPZ. It was a joy to work alongside them in these efforts to bring Zairians a more abundant life.

With the women's choir after being made an honorary member

We had been studying Hebrews in our daily devotions towards the end of 1990. On January 1, 1991, Bill said that he felt God was saying Hebrews 12:1–2 should be our theme verses for the new year. As the year progressed, I added verse 3. I like the way Eugene Petersen translates it in *The Message*:

> *Do you see what this means—all these pioneers who blazed the way, all these veterans cheering us on? It means we'd better get on with it. Strip down, start running—and never quit! No extra spiritual fat, no parasitic sins. Keep your eyes on <u>Jesus</u>, who both began and finished the race we're in. Study how he did it. Because he never lost sight of where he was headed—that exhilarating finish in and with God—he could put up with anything along the way: cross, shame, whatever. And now he's <u>there</u>, in the place of honor, right alongside God. When you find yourself flagging in your faith, go over that story again, item by item, that long litany of hostility he plowed through. That will shoot adrenaline into your souls.*

Little did we know how important these verses would become in the year ahead.

There were price changes now several times a day in the grocery stores. Banks had been closed for more than a year and cash was not easily accessible in the country. The Zaire currency was devaluing rapidly. Fifty dollars U.S. changed into a table full of Zaires. Bill was particularly under stress at this time because he needed to buy building materials so that Badibanga and his construction crew could continue to work. Project money was available, of course, from Alex Booth, The Outreach Foundation, and the PC(USA). However, we had to spend a great deal of time and energy getting our money changed into Zaires. This was no easy task because we had to count and recount whatever we were given. Bill was very conscious of being a good steward of the funds. Prices fluctuated so greatly that Bill had to bargain daily for the cheapest prices for wood, cement, iron bars, roofing sheets, etc. I was serving on the board of Habitat for Humanity in Kinshasa, so Bill and I got to know many of the Habitat staff. They also were working on construction projects, mostly houses. Bill was able to help them find cheaper prices for their materials.

On February 14, Bill went out to pick up an order of wood. Somehow, while loading our car, he lifted it the wrong way and injured his back. The doctor prescribed rest and put Bill on muscle relaxants and pain medication to help him sleep and ordered him *not to lift anything*. Of course, Bill wanted to get up and be involved in construction and other projects but, thankfully, our son William was living with us at that time and teaching at TASOK. He was a great help. William and I kept things going. We were so thankful for Badibanga and all he was doing. Bill became increasingly concerned he might have to have back surgery. A wonderful young Baptist missionary physician, who played tennis with William, examined Bill and recommended that he needed to get out of his stressful environment in order to heal, but added that he was not convinced Bill would need to have surgery. We were thankful for his words of encouragement.

Finally, after nearly six weeks, the doctors convinced Bill to return to the States. We flew on Luftansa Airlines to Frankfurt and then changed to a Delta flight. That plane caught fire, but fortunately within thirty minutes of the pilot's announcement, we were able to set down in Newfoundland. God was certainly watching over us!

When we arrived at the airport, people on the ground were not prepared for a 747 with three hundred passengers. We sat on the plane for more than an hour while the fire crew boarded in their masks and other regalia to check things out. Bill and I had not been worried about the problem, although he did get frustrated because, once the crew realized the plane was on fire, they turned off the movie, and he never got to see the ending.

Bill had not wanted me to request a wheelchair, but I had already told the crew about his back problems. When we were finally allowed to deplane, we were told there were only a few hotel rooms available, to be offered first to women, children, and those who were infirm. Bill needed to lie down, so I requested a room, but we offered to share it with another couple, because it had two queen beds. Not many people requested rooms, so no one ever took us up on the offer. As it turned out, March Madness had begun. The NCAA basketball games were on TV, so Bill forgave me for speaking up and requesting a room. After a layover of sixteen hours, we boarded another plane for Atlanta, where we were greeted with news headlines in the U.S. about the Delta plane that had caught fire. Again, we thanked God for his protection and for a safe arrival at home.

After consulting with Dr. Brown Dennis, a caring friend and excellent doctor, and a neurologist he recommended, it was decided that Bill could go on to Orlando to rest and recuperate at my mother's home. In Orlando, Bill met with another neurologist who told him surgery might not be needed. He sent Bill to a sports clinic where he was given daily exercises. Within six weeks, Bill was deemed well enough for us to return to Zaire. We arrived in May 1991 in time for the Centennial celebration of Presbyterian mission work in Zaire.

Celebration and Crisis

The beginning of the Presbyterian mission in the Belgian Congo is an interesting story. In 1891, the Rev. Samuel Lapsley, a white pastor from Alabama, and Rev. William H. Sheppard, a black pastor from Virginia, were appointed to be the first two Presbyterian missionaries to go to the Belgian Congo. To me it is wonderful that our Presbyterian work there started by sending out an integrated team of missionaries. That fact was much appreciated by the Congolese people. The two men were not used to the conditions in Congo; within three years Samuel Lapsley had contracted a fever and died, but William Sheppard survived, had a family, and continued his work for twenty more years. Other missionaries came. Malaria was rampant, along with other diseases, and many missionaries died, especially women and children. It was a difficult time with a great deal of sacrifice and suffering under harsh conditions. When there was war or outbreak of disease, the men would send their families out of the area or back to the U.S., so that missionary families were often separated for long periods of time. Yet they felt a strong call to share the Gospel with the Congolese people, to train disciples and church leaders, to heal, and to educate.

The May 1991 celebration of the 100-year anniversary of Presbyterian missionaries arriving in Congo was planned by the CPK (Presbyterian Church of Kinshasa) and CPZ (Presbyterian Church of Zaire). Dr. Cliff Kirkpatrick, PC(USA) Director of International Missions, came along with Dr. Yen Whitney and a few others from the denominational office. Bill and I were glad we had returned in time to celebrate this historic event. Several churches in Kinshasa held special services to thank God for the arrival of Sheppard and Lapsley in 1891 and the beginning of the Presbyterian mission work. Worship services included choirs, dancing and singing, as well as celebrative meals. Then we flew up-country to Kananga and enjoyed participating in more centennial celebrations. We traveled together over some terrible roads to get to Lake Munkamba and Mbuji Mayi and continue the commemoration, but the fellowship and joyful worship services were very special.

At that time, we were living in Limeté, the same section of Kinshasa where Mobutu's opposition leader, Etienne Tshisekedi, lived. Even though the President had declared an end to single party rule and the start of democracy on April 24, 1990, democracy was in name only. Mobutu repeatedly had Tshisekedi put under house arrest. When Bill and I passed Tshisekedi's house on our early morning walks, he would come out and wave to us from the porch, and the military guards who were keeping him under house arrest also waved to us. Many of these guards were Christians and knew we were missionaries. Bill and I laughed that only in Zaire would the opposition leader be under house arrest, unable to leave the country, and yet we could be friendly with him and with those who were guarding him, because we all loved the Lord Jesus Christ.

We thanked God for the fellowship and concern of our Presbyterians sisters and brothers in Kinshasa, especially those in Limeté who made up the Presbyterian Community of Kinshasa. They checked on us and kept us informed when there was a problem downtown, at the airport, or elsewhere in the city, warning us not to go into town if they'd heard that there might be a demonstration or possibility of violence. One afternoon as we were out walking, we got caught up in a demonstration near Tshisekedi's house. When we saw police gathering, we knew to run in the other direction. The police and riot squad were readily available to clamp down on any protest.

On Monday morning, September 28, all hell broke loose in Kinshasa. It became known as "the pillage." We had been warned over the weekend by our Zairian friends to stay home because something was brewing. The turmoil started about three o'clock in the morning, and soon rioting and pillaging had spread all over town. The military had finally revolted because Mobutu hadn't paid them. We didn't know what was happening, but we heard that planes couldn't take off or land because the international airport was "out of order." We thought the military had dug a hole in the concrete, but instead they had parked planes on the runways, blocking all air traffic. Downtown, the military and the crowds following them destroyed about ninety percent of the business district.

We stayed in our house most of the day. William was across town at TASOK. We were aware there were problems over there, but we figured the school would be okay. We knew U.S. Ambassador Melissa Wells kept track of all of us Americans and had a plan for us to gather at certain safe places. There were no places to gather in Limeté, but we had a CB radio and the embassy had asked us to call in if there was any danger.

That morning a crowd of angry people came up our street, and we saw that our next-door neighbor's house was being taken apart. The crowd violently pulled the wife and husband out. The soldiers didn't wind up hurting them, but the couple was traumatized, and their house was destroyed, even though our neighbors were business people and not involved in politics. We weren't sure what was going to happen, so we closed our curtains and prayed that Odie, our German Shepherd, wouldn't bark and call attention to us. We formed a circle with our cook, Tata Mata, and our foreman, Badibanga, along with several others on Badibanga's team, and we prayed that things would quiet down all over town. I don't know if the turmoil was orchestrated to happen all at once, but it was like an explosion of anger and bitterness overflowing into the streets. That day Tata Mata prayed for Bill and me saying, "Lord, protect these people from injury. They've come here to work with us, and we love them." And then Bill and I prayed for each of them and their families because they didn't know what was happening in their neighborhoods.

By four o'clock that afternoon things had quieted down. The guards felt Bill and I should not go out, so one of them went around the corner to the home of Bill Simmons, another Presbyterian missionary. Bill was out of the country and his wife, Willie, wasn't home. It was decided that we should not spend the night in our house, because the crowd had been down our street and might come back. There was a telephone and better protection at the Simmons' house. We drove there in our Land Rover taking only our passports and bare necessities. The next day people from the embassy warned us that it was time for us to come to one of the designated safe places. Bill and Judy Young, another PC(USA) missionary couple, had already arrived at the ambassador's house and encouraged us to come. "We've got a pool, the TASOK kids are here, and it isn't all that crowded," they reported. We knew we would have to pray and make a decision soon as to where to go. Bill and I didn't feel unsafe, even though the Simmons' house was on the main road into town, but we made the decision to go to the ambassador's residence.

Bill and I got little sleep that night. The next morning, we began to make our plans. It was decided that I, as a white woman, probably should not be visible. One of Pastor Tshimungu's sons who worked for the Simmons family put boxes inside our Land Rover for me to hide under, and we headed out. Cars filled the streets, one after another, loaded down with stolen goods, even some with a refrigerator on top. It was like a scene from a banana republic movie.

Military men in dark glasses drove around making the V-for-victory sign and hanging out of cars, obviously stolen. Stores were being looted and burned; people were taking whatever they could.

Pastor Jibikelayi told Bill to act like he was a pastor (which, of course, he was) if we were stopped. We didn't know if they

With Ambassador Melissa Wells

were stopping expats. We didn't know what was really going on. I hid on the floor of the Land Rover with boxes on top of me. Jibikelayi was leaning out and driving as if he were one of those wild people who had stolen the boxes. As we drove along, I could hear Bill saying, "Oh my goodness, oh gracious." There was destruction and devastation everywhere. One of the large department stores was being burned as we passed. It looked as if the city had been bombed, but it hadn't. There were crowds of people breaking windows, destroying property, and stealing whatever they could carry off. Papers and litter were strewn everywhere. In some instances, there were computers outside on the ground. During our twenty-minute drive, it was astounding to see how much damage had been done in just two days. There were three or four cars traveling in our group, and ours was the lead car. We each had CB radios, so we could communicate.

Finally, we arrived at the U.S. Ambassador Melissa Wells' residence. French and Belgian paratroopers had already come into the country, and on Tuesday the French Foreign Legion parachuted in. They were picking up missionaries from the interior and bringing them to a small airport. Several of these missionaries were parents of children at the Methodist-Presbyterian Youth Hostel, and they didn't know what was going on. By the time we all arrived, there were about twenty of us staying at the ambassador's house. The hostel had brought food so we had something to eat. The ambassador had stored mattresses to offer us, but she also had a lovely couch in her living room. Our group decided they would give me the couch if I would answer the phone. Ambassador Wells said she needed to try to get some sleep because it had been a wild time for two days, and she felt if she didn't get some rest, she wouldn't be able to think clearly. The French and Belgian Ambassadors, the British High Commission, and the Americans were working in tandem, and she said if the phone rang—her red phone—to knock on her door. I felt uncomfortable, because that was her bedroom door where she and her husband slept, but I said, "If I get the couch, I can do that!" A call did come in the middle of the second night, and I did knock on her door.

Ambassador Wells spent some time with me, and we joked to-gether. Everyone was telling her I was a Democrat, and I knew she was a Republican. She was an impressive person, a career ambassa-dor, and a wonderful lady. We stayed at her residence from Tuesday until Thursday. On Tuesday when we arrived, we had a special time of fellowship; then on Wednesday, there was indecision. The am-bassador said her office was suggesting that we leave the country, but they weren't ordering us to do so. Bill talked about staying and William wanted to stay, but I thought I would go on back to the U.S. By Thursday, however, we'd all made the decision to leave the country. The ambassador told us, "Okay, my understanding is that ferry boats will come for all of you. We'll have buses to pick you up." There were about ten thousand Westerners who needed to be evacuated: missionaries of many denominations, Peace Corps vol-unteers, U.S. embassy personnel, and many others, including Jane Goodall. The Embassy made plans for us to go across the Zaire River to Brazzaville.

There were sixty-eight PC(USA) missionaries and family mem-bers. Ambassador Wells told us if we'd like to return to our houses and get anything that was valuable to us, we would be allowed one suitcase, but we had to be back by five o'clock. So, Bill drove the truck with William and me to Limeté. A group of about eight sol-diers with guns over their shoulders were at the turn of the road near our house. They held their hands up for us to stop. Bill told me to lock the back doors. The soldiers very politely asked if we were going further out. When we said yes but not far, they asked for a ride. Bill didn't feel he could say no, so they climbed into the back of the truck. We could hear them talking to each other. They did not seem to be arrogant or appear as if they had been drinking. When we got to the turn to go right onto our street, Bill stopped the truck and told them this was as far as we were going. We wondered what would happen next. Incredibly, they got down from the truck and said, "Thank you, Pastor." That surprised us. We don't know how they knew Bill was a pastor, but they waved and went on their way. They could have commandeered the truck and left us high and dry, but instead they acknowledged we were Christians and missionaries. We thanked God for this encounter and went on to our house.

We already had a packed suitcase with our passports and medicines, but we had less than an hour to decide what else was most valuable to take with us. I gathered some pictures; William had some artwork he had collected. Before we had left the ambassador's house, we had asked the kitchen staff what we could bring them. They asked for Bibles. Bill went out back and got several Bibles. We made sure all our pets had food and had someone to take care of them. Thankfully, Tata Mata was still around. Then we locked the house and drove back to the ambassador's residence. Once there, we distributed Bibles to soldiers, kitchen staff, and to all who had helped us. We had a good meal, the kids swam in the pool, and we had a time of fellowship and prayer.

The following day the buses came for us. William was a great help loading suitcases for those who were not able to lift them. As we left, our last view of the ambassador's residence was of the guards sitting at the gate reading their new Bibles. I still get chill bumps thinking about it. Some of them had probably not owned a Bible previously so it was very touching to see them reading God's Word in the midst of their country falling apart.

One very disturbing event happened as we passed the U.S. Embassy. We saw an American who had been head of the CIA in Zaire. He was rumored to be very close with Mobutu and was notorious for enriching himself with diamonds. We observed that the embassy personnel ended up turning over all the keys to him.

Our buses drove down to the Zaire River where we were loaded onto a ferry. As we pulled away and saw the outline of the tall buildings of Kinshasa, many of us began to cry. I cried, but I also said a prayer of gratitude to God for all that had been accomplished during the seven years Bill and I had been back in Zaire. What a privilege it had been to work with Elder Badibanga to help build churches, manses and schools, and to train pastors, evangelists and lay leaders. We were thankful for Alex Booth's generous donations, for The Outreach Foundation, the PC(USA), and all who had helped make this possible. These had been productive years. As the ferry pulled away, many of us wondered if we would ever be back.

Once we arrived in Brazzaville, we were called refugees. We were to fly out on the planes that are used for various missions when there is a crisis. These planes had just been used in Bosnia to fly out embassy personnel. The crew was trained for crisis situations and they were enormously helpful. There were over four hundred people on our plane. William and a friend had brought a little Kahlua and asked for milk to mix with it. After carrying all that luggage, they were worn out. I have a precious picture of them fast asleep soon after our departure.

**Bill, William and I as we wait for the ferry
to evacuate from Kinshasa**

The flight home was not exactly a time of mourning because many of us thought that once we got home the U.S. would see what had happened and would understand that the policy of support for Mobutu was wrong. We had high expectations that maybe this up-heaval had to happen in order for people to see how evil Mobutu was and how much the people of Zaire were suffering. The military and the trained mercenaries were the ones who rioted, because they had not been paid. Eighteen hundred French and Belgian troops had calmed down a city of five-and-a-half-million. These soldiers let it be known there was a curfew at 5:30 p.m. and anyone on the streets after that time would be shot. One paratrooper was killed, but I don't think any other people died. It was still traumatic, however, as a lot of our Zairian friends lost their homes and property when the military went on rampages. We missionaries were able to go back to our homeland, but the Zairian people we had come to know and love were in the midst of having their homeland destroyed.

On the plane we shared stories. One was about our foreman, Badibanga, who was building a Presbyterian school and had a pile of rocks and building supplies in the schoolyard. A mob of people came by and threatened to take the building materials. Badibanga replied that the materials were not his, they were God's. They had been purchased by Presbyterians to build a school for Zairian children. Upon hearing this, the mob left him alone and went on down the street. One thing was evident from the stories they shared: the military had revolted against Mobutu and those who were helping him build his kingdom, but they didn't bother those who were working and helping to build God's kingdom.

Once we reached U.S. soil, we were no longer refugees. We were taken to Andrews Air Force Base where Cliff Kirkpatrick and the number two officer in the Air Force, a Presbyterian, came to meet us. They were allowed to come out on the tarmac and greet us as we descended from the plane. We laughed that the Presbyterians outdid even the Baptists this time in having the first contact.

Bill and I had evacuated with two Zairian children. While we were still at the ambassador's house in Kinshasa, Elder Mbote Tshek, a family friend, had asked us to take his children to an aunt living in the U.S. The two children, a teenage girl and her younger brother, were born in the United States while Tshek was studying here. He had received permission from the U.S. embassy to send the children with us. When we got to the U.S., the children did not want to leave us. They were caught between two worlds: their parents in Kinshasa and their U.S. aunt whom they had not seen for years. It was a very painful time for them, but fortunately their family was able to follow them to the U.S. a few months later.

After our evacuation, we moved to Mission Haven in Decatur, Georgia. We were glad to be close to Bill's family once again. Sadly, shortly after we returned, Bill's father, Lucian, was diagnosed with terminal cancer. Although we had not wanted to be evacuated, it was very special for Bill to have time with his father before he died.

Upon our arrival in the U.S., we got to a phone and called my mother and Shamba in Orlando. The State Department had already called them. Not much news had been reported in the U.S. about all the turmoil in Zaire, so the fact that they received a call really frightened them. The third largest country in Africa, bordering on nine countries and right in the heart of Africa, was coming apart, and our news media did not see fit to cover the story. Most people did not seem to know or care about Zaire. I was upset and concerned.

Our friend Henri Rush encouraged me to use my anger and concern to become an advocate, to speak out. Henri was a lawyer and an elder at Westminster Presbyterian Church in Alexandria, Virginia. He had visited us several times in Zaire, once with his wife Candace. Bill and I had become close friends with Henri and Candace and stayed with them when visiting in D.C.

Our daughter, Elizabeth, had worked for *Africa News* for four years while she was at Duke University. The two editors, husband and wife Reed Kramer and Tami Hultman, contacted her and asked if she knew anyone among the missionaries who would speak out about the situation in Zaire. Of course, she knew of one: "Yes! My mother!" They began running interviews with me. I thanked them for caring and told them that when you're not living in Zaire and seeing how the people suffer, it's easy to act as though not much is happening. I felt the riots and destruction that had just occurred were the final straw. Mobutu was evil; his own countrymen, as well as we missionaries, wanted him gone.

Five weeks after our evacuation, the PC(USA) Division of International Mission brought the sixty-eight missionary families, including children, together at a Catholic retreat center near Nashville. We spent three or four days sharing stories, talking, and praying with the Louisville staff who were meeting with us. Several people who had been through other crises came to pray with us and to hear our cries. I clearly felt God urging me to continue to speak out. God had been preparing me for such a task; I had the background and experience.

My friend Art Simon—founder of Bread for the World, author, Lutheran minister, and the brother of Senator Paul Simon—had told me he would help me if I ever wanted to speak with Senator Simon, Chairman of the Senate Foreign Relations African Subcommittee. So, I called him. Things were desperate in Zaire, and we had heard the French Foreign Legion was planning to leave very soon. There would be chaos in Kinshasa again. Zairians wanted the French to stay, but Mobutu wanted them out. Art told me to be prepared for the senator's call and to know exactly what I wanted to say, because I wouldn't have much time to talk to him. I had already spoken (and cried) with the other missionaries, and together we decided on four or five things we felt were important to communicate to the senator and other members of the Senate Foreign Relations Subcommittee.

When Senator Simon called, I had just five minutes to share what we Presbyterian missionaries wanted to say. I thanked him for his concern and then we hung up. His top aide, Adwoa Dunn, called me right back and asked if Senator Simon had asked me to testify at the hearing on Zaire in D.C. on Nov. 6, 1991, which was the next week. I replied that I didn't know about the hearing, and she said she would speak to the senator. Apparently, he agreed that I should be on the public panel. I was the only one testifying who had been evacuated. We learned from National Public Radio ahead of the hearing that Herman Cohen, Assistant Secretary of State for African Affairs, was going to recommend that Mobutu be left in power. We felt that would be a devastating decision for our sisters and brothers in Zaire. I remember that I cried, and then Bill and I started to work on what I would say. Our family, along with other missionaries and friends, were praying for me.

I would have only five minutes to speak at the hearing. I learned from Henri Rush that four and a half minutes into my testimony a yellow light would appear, and at five minutes a red light would come on. It is possible for the committee chair to give a speaker an additional minute or two if they want, but this extra time is not assured. Henri helped me as I prepared my testimony on the situation in Zaire to fit the short time frame. This was the first public hearing of the Subcommittee on African Affairs of the Foreign Relations Committee to be held since Mobutu had been put into power twenty-six years ago. I knew of three senators who would be there for the hearing: Nancy Kassebaum from Kansas, Chairman Paul Simon from Illinois, and Richard Lugar from Indiana. Also in the room were some friends, Dr. Yen Whitney from PC(USA), Henri Rush, and several Zairians. I knew many more were praying for me.

Assistant Secretary Cohen gave the first statement after Senator Simon opened the hearing. I felt Herman Cohen spoke in a very uncaring manner as he said he thought the U.S. should leave Mobutu in the mix because he still had a political role to play. As he said this I started to cry, but I felt several hands of reassurance on my shoulders, some of them Zairians. That gave me strength.

After I spoke, Senator Simon quizzed me a bit and then asked me to make my closing remarks. My closing comments were on the final page, so I quickly flipped pages to get to them. I thanked the U.S. government for bringing us home and said we were grateful for the support we'd had from the Presbyterian Church. Unlike many refugees, we had not been abandoned and were coming back to a safe haven and a wonderful place. But I strongly urged them to cut our ties with Mobutu and publicly denounce him. Two others on the panel, Peter Rosenblum with the Lawyers Committee for Human Rights and Dr. Herbert Weiss, professor of political science at Brooklyn College, also spoke against Mobutu. Then Senator Simon asked, "Mrs. Warlick, if indeed the U.S. government decided to publicly denounce Mobutu, how would that word get out?" I answered, "Senator, it could be put on BBC, CNN, and Voice of America. These statements don't need to be made too loudly; they will resound." Some of the people in the audience clapped. Several people told me I was the most passionate person on the panel.

Because my family and I had lived there and knew how much the people were suffering, I couldn't approach the problems from a strictly academic basis. At the end of the hearing, Andy Semmel, Senator Lugar's staff person for Foreign Relations, waved at me and then handed me a note that the senator had been moved by my testimony. Later he told me that Senator Lugar had been hearing about the terrible situation in Zaire from several missionaries: Mennonites, Methodists, Presbyterians, Baptists, and others. The senator told Andy that when missionaries begin calling your office, you'd better listen! Tim Trenkle, Foreign Relations staff person in Senator Kassebaum's office, thanked me and later said that he told Assistant Secretary Cohen that his testimony was watered down and Cohen replied, "Clearly, it was a wimpy speech!" The news media quoted both Simon and Kassebaum as disagreeing with Cohen's testimony. Senator Simon asked the Bush administration to persuade Mobutu to leave Zaire, at least for a period, after turning power over to an interim government.

After the hearing, Dr. William Close, Mobutu's personal physician for sixteen years, got in touch with me. (Interestingly, he is the father of Glenn Close, the movie actress.) Although we had never met in Zaire, we ended up working together with Sen. Simon and his staff to try to get the White House to cut ties with Mobutu. Obviously, Bill Close knew Mobutu very well and had a wealth of personal information about the dictator.

In the weeks and months that followed, I attended further hearings in D.C. and spoke at several of them. On November 23, 1991, *The Atlanta Constitution* ran a key article, "Standing Up to Evil," by Deborah Scroggins. From our interview, she quoted me as saying, "I just want my government to do what is morally and ethically right: break ties with this man who personifies evil." I kept hoping that the Bush administration would publicly condemn Mobutu for his misrule and the atrocities against his people and that the U.S. would cut any ties we had with him. The House of Representatives passed a resolution urging Mobutu to step down, but the Senate never ratified it. This was a huge disappointment to me and many others.

During this time, I was mentioned in a couple of Christian magazines. I was said to be "hounding the members of the Bush administration" in one and "badgering the members of U.S. Congress" in another. It became a joke and several of my friends called me the hound and the badger. Henri Rush gave me a china badger figurine which I still have. Representative Harry Johnson (D-FL) was the chair of the Africa Sub-committee in the House. He became a good friend. As he would see me coming down the hall and going into his office, he would say, "Here comes Mrs. Warlick, so I know we're going to talk about Zaire." He worked very hard to get the House of Representatives to pass the resolution.

In December 1993, John Metzel, a son of Presbyterian missionaries, went to D.C. with me to meet with the staffs of Senators Simon, Lugar, and Kassebaum. In addition, following violence in Kananga, we went to the White House to speak about the worsening situation in Zaire. During the years 1991–1994, Senator Simon was my hero. He really cared about Africa. He asked the Bush (41) administration to persuade Mobutu to step down because Mobutu had lost the legitimacy to govern Zaire. Senators Kassebaum and Lugar joined Senator Simon in speaking out about what was happening in Zaire. It was a privilege to have worked with these caring U.S. senators and their staff members. In January 1994, after President Clinton's inauguration, we met with Ambassador Jennifer Ward, the African Advisor to the National Security Council. She wanted the Clinton Administration to break ties with Mobutu.

In February 1994, there was a USAID roundtable discussion held at the State Department concerning the worsening humanitarian crisis in Zaire. Amnesty International put out a report entitled, "Zaire, Collapsing Under Crisis." Sadly, for the Zairian people, however, Mobutu remained in power for a few more years. Finally, in 1996 he really began to lose his grip and eventually lost the presidency. Mobutu had caused much destruction and suffering for his people in the years he ruled. It was heartbreaking to know that he left the country and its citizens in such terrible shape.

Zimbabwe Bound

We moved to Louisville, Kentucky, where Bill and I served as Missionaries-in-Residence with the Presbyterian Global Mission office from the end of 1991 until June 1994. It was a joy to be in the States when our daughter Elizabeth married Dan Turk January 8th, 1994. During these years, we kept very busy. While I was advocating for justice for the Zairian people, Bill helped coordinate evangelism projects in Africa together with the Revs. Mort Taylor and Jeff Ritchie in the International Evangelism office.

Because of my advocacy and speaking out against President Mobutu, we could not return to Zaire. Bill made a trip to several other countries in southern Africa in 1992. Then in the fall of 1993, we were asked to go to Harare, the capital of Zimbabwe, to visit projects in Malawi, Zimbabwe and Zambia. We jumped at the chance. It was wonderful to be back on African soil and to visit with PC(USA) missionaries Rev. Dave and Polly Miller, who were based in Harare. We met African sisters and brothers in the area and felt God's call to serve in southern Africa. By April 1994, we were able to send a newsletter that announced our new assignment, to be based in Harare:

> *"The joy that the Lord gives you will make you strong" (Neh. 8:10). Our big news is that we will be moving to Harare, Zimbabwe in August 1994 to continue to work in the Project of Evangelism and Church Growth in Africa (PECGA). This is the tenth year for this project. We will be coordinating PECGA in five southern African countries: Zimbabwe, Zambia, Malawi, Mozambique, and Madagascar.*

By November 1994, we were overjoyed to be settled in, living again in Africa. Visiting with church leaders in Malawi, Zambia and Zimbabwe reminded us of both the joys and the difficulties facing

Africans today. A Ghanaian proverb says, "If you want someone to help you lift a load to your head, you must first lift it to your knees." We found a lot of people in southern Africa who had lifted loads to their knees and now needed help in lifting these loads to their heads in order to be in position to move ahead. As African Christians were seeking to live out their faith daily in the midst of harsh circumstances, we witnessed once again the vitality of the growing church on that continent. "The fullness of joy is to behold God in everything"[iii] is a favorite quote of mine. Certainly our African brothers and sisters in Christ *do* see that God is with them in the midst of adversity. Again, we were made aware of how much we can learn from them about joy and being strong in all situations.

In northern Malawi, a group of remarkable young Christians sang for us at the Ekwendeni Center near Mzuzu. They were all blind! Yet they ministered to us in a special way that morning as they sang joyfully, *Father, I adore you, lay my life before you, how I love you.* We were touched by their Christian dedication and commitment. Although physically blind, they certainly displayed great discernment and spiritual insight. The presence of Christ was so real to them. The Church of Central Africa (CCAP) is reaching out in ministry to these blind young people, giving them a place to live and go to school. They are helping the blind to see!

During our first month in Harare we were without a car, but we lived close enough to the downtown area to walk. As we trekked daily into town to pick up our mail, buy groceries, go to the bank and various other errands, we sometimes stepped around children on the street who were sleeping, begging, or just sitting on the curb. Some of them had sniffed glue and were "stoned." How horrifying it was to see the conditions in which these children lived and "worked." After several days we got to know some of them. I remember Nshingi, a precious little boy who had been on the streets just a short time. He was such a loving child. Later, we were able to reunite him with his grandmother.

I also remember Noel, one of the first kids I got to know. He was a winsome, outgoing boy of about nine or ten. His mother was alive, and they had a place to sleep about an hour away in Chitungweza. His grandmother was blind. Unfortunately, these two women used Noel and his brother and sisters to beg. Much later, we found out that his mother and sisters were prostitutes. Noel was engaging, streetwise, and very smart. Naturally, he knew Shona, the language used by seventy-five percent of the people in Zimbabwe, but he also spoke English quite well. Noel came up to Bill and me one day and told us he was hungry. I asked Noel what he would like to have to eat. We often gave bread, bananas, and hard-boiled eggs to the children. That day, however, Noel said he wanted to go to the grocery store because his mother and his family needed some food. I decided to take him to a local grocery store and thought I'd spend about fifteen dollars. He picked out several items—oil, flour, sugar, meat, milk, tea—things his family would need. I said, "Noel you haven't gotten anything for yourself. What would you like?" He said, "I'd like some yogurt." I replied, "Great. Let's get some yogurt."

As he sat and ate two or three cups of yogurt, he told me some of his story. "Nancy, I do go to school. I'm in grade three. I like going to school, but one of the problems is I don't have a school uniform." Children in Zimbabwe, even in public school, wear school uniforms, which can be expensive for a family with limited funds. If a student does not wear a uniform, it is obvious to his classmates that he is from a poor family, so they call him a "street kid," a derogatory term. When I asked Noel how often he went to school, he told me he went every day. I said, "Noel, it's hard for me to believe you go every day because we see you here downtown so often." He said, "Well, I go in the mornings, and I come into town in the afternoon."

I was really drawn to Noel and decided he would be one of the children I would try to get to know better. He said he went to church and that he would like to go to church with me some time. I told him I'd love to have him go to church with me, but I thought it would be better for him to attend church near where his mother and grandmother were staying. I felt that he and his younger brother didn't need to keep coming into downtown Harare where they could get into trouble. He was such a cute, bright-eyed boy that it was obvious someone could take advantage of him and persuade him to steal or be involved in even worse problems. He told me what he really wanted most of all was to have a school uniform. After talking further with him, I said, "Okay, if you will go to school every day next week, then I will meet you and we'll get a school uniform." He was so excited. Then I suggested that we have a Bible study somewhere, and we went that afternoon to Harare Gardens, a local park. Noel knew a lot of Bible stories and said he loved Jesus Christ. He promised to go to school every day the next week. We prayed together, and I gave him some coins to ride the bus home with his little brother.

A few days later the car Bill and I had ordered arrived, a Nissan Patrol, so we did not walk into town as often. However, at the end of the week I met Noel as promised in Harare Gardens.

With Noel (l) and Moses (r), two boys who were part of the street children ministry

This park was not a very safe place, but the kids who were on their own liked to go there. So, I met Noel and we went to Woolworth's department store and got his uniform. I asked him, "Noel, how will I know you are going to school?" He said, "Oh, Nancy, I love to go to school! You don't need to worry." The next time I went downtown in the afternoon Noel was there, but he again said he was going to school in the morning and coming into town afterwards. He also said he didn't have any shoes. I decided a boy going to school did need shoes, so we went shopping once more. For about five dollars, I found him a pair of school shoes and some knee socks.

Not long after that, I wrote about Noel in a newsletter that Bill and I sent to our church supporters.

Noel is a very bright ten-year-old who spends hours each day on the streets of Harare begging for money and food. He is one of thousands of children who are helping to keep their families going by 'hustling' on the streets, trying to eke out an existence. Noel is unusual because he goes to school for part of each day before coming to town to beg. He is actually a remarkable child in many other ways. He has been begging for some time, but he doesn't sniff glue (as many his age do). He is very helpful and polite. I first met him one afternoon several months ago outside of a department store when he told me he was hungry. I bought him something to eat and we talked. We have become friends since then. He is extremely intelligent and gifted in languages. In trying to help Noel, we have found that his home situation is quite sad. His father has died. His mother had help from one of her brothers, but he recently died as well. She used to crochet items to sell across the border. However, she has not been able to do this recently. We found that the five children live with her in a very small, dingy room. She was behind in her rent of $15 a month. We were able to pay for three months' back rent so that she wasn't evicted. We are now trying to help her return to crocheting items so that she can have something to sell to help feed her children.

Meanwhile, we have talked to her about the fact that Noel and his little brother are spending late hours on the streets. Two of her other children are in school also, but they won't smile. Noel says he loves Jesus and is always eager to sing Bible choruses and dance during our weekly meetings with some of the children in crisis (as we prefer to call the street children) at City Presbyterian Church in downtown Harare. We have given Noel school shoes recently. When I saw him last week in the cold without shoes, I asked him where his shoes were. He responded with wisdom beyond his years, "Nancy, I have to leave my shoes at home and wear them only to school. That way they will last longer." Then he gave me one of his sparkling smiles. I wanted to cry, but I smiled in return. I told him that he was very smart, but I really wanted to shout that no ten-year-old child should have to make that kind of a decision. I pray a lot for Noel and his family. I am concerned about what the future holds for him.

We had been living in Harare about two months when Bill and I met Maury Mendenhall, a young lady from Texas who was studying at the University of Zimbabwe during her junior year in college. As part of an independent project, she was volunteering with ten or twelve street children for six months. We had known Maury's parents, the Rev. Drs. Chuck and Laura Mendenhall, in Congo when they spent a year in 1971 as Presbyterian mission volunteers. They had told us Maury was coming to Harare. We soon found out that Noel was one of the children in Maury's project. She was very fond of him. After talking with Maury, we decided that one or two days a week we would meet kids in Harare Gardens and play games and do art projects with them. We enjoyed doing fun activities that the kids couldn't do on their own, because they didn't have such things as crayons or paper. We sang and laughed together. Maury involved them in dramatic skits and also had them sketch what they wanted to do when they grew up. I agreed to teach a Bible story and we sang Bible songs. One song they especially enjoyed singing was "There's No One Like Jesus," a traditional African song. They had motions to go along with the words:

> *There's no one, there's no one like Jesus; There's no one, there's no one like him. (repeat 2x)*
>
> *I walk and walk here and there; I search and search here and there.*
>
> *I turn around everywhere. There's no one, there's no one like him.*

Maury and the kids told us about a compassionate lady named Joan Trevelyan, known as the Tea and Bread Lady, because she served children hot tea with milk and bread early each morning, Monday through Friday, downtown by the Anglican Cathedral where she was a member. The bishop would not let her feed the kids on the church grounds because on one occasion the children had blocked his parking place. Joan had been working with children on the streets since 1989, and the children called her *Mabau*, the Shona word for "loved one."

The first time I met Joan, I found her with her son, Craig, feeding the children. As we talked, we discovered that we were next-door neighbors. What a blessing to live so close to Joan! I learned that she had started helping the children when they kept asking her to take them to a nearby shop for tea and bread. Eventually, going to the shop so often got expensive, and Joan began bringing three loaves of her own bread and some tea for the kids. She started simply, and her ministry grew from that small beginning to make a huge difference. Often the work was discouraging, but Joan said, "God tells me every day not to be overwhelmed."

We learned quite a lot from Joan as we began to work with her to help needy kids. She has had suffering in her life, yet the Dostovesky quote, "the soul is healed by being with children," is true for Joan. She is one of the most compassionate people we have ever met. To this day, she is one of our most cherished friends.

I realized God truly had a plan for taking care of these precious, needy children and that God was calling Bill and me to join in a ministry with Joan to help redeem these children and get them off the streets. From that day forward in December 1994, we began to work and pray together for God's leading. We wanted the children to have an abundant life in Christ. We knew they were leading unhealthy and destructive lives. John Stott wrote, "Vision begins with a holy discontent with things as they are." Slowly our vision for the children began to take form.

In early December, Maury decided she'd like to spend Christmas with some of the kids we had met. Bill and I agreed to help her. She invited several other students from the U.S. who were studying at the University to participate. We had none of our immediate family with us, so we threw ourselves into the preparations and enjoyment of this event. City Presbyterian Church, located downtown, allowed us to decorate and use a room for a Christmas Eve supper. Maury and a few other American university students asked the Monomatapa Hotel nearby to donate the food. The students also rented a room in a local youth hostel for the night. They put up a Christmas tree with lights and let the kids make ornaments. The dingy fifteen-by-fifteen foot room came alive with a poster-board fireplace and festive decorations. Ten or so mattresses were on the floor. Bill and I brought our TV and VCR so the kids could enjoy watching *The Grinch Who Stole Christmas, Beauty and the Beast,* and the *Jesus Film*, which they watched from beginning to end. The kids said they liked the *Jesus Film* the best!

Early Christmas morning, Bill and I went back to the hostel to pick up the TV, VCR, and some other supplies, and then attended worship at City Presbyterian Church with some of the children. Afterwards, the kids went back to the street with a lunch bag and warm feelings about the meaning and love of Christmas. The kids were very appreciative and kept thanking us for spending Christmas with them. It was certainly the most unusual Christmas we had ever spent! Out of this experience, we grew closer to these children and continued to find out more and more about their hard lives on the streets. We became deeply committed to share with them the love of Jesus in word and deed.

Joan knew Noel and all of the kids at our Christmas party because they came to have tea and bread with her in the mornings. She fed them very early, about 6:30 or 7:00 a.m. I soon found out from Joan that Noel often did sleep on the streets because he was there for tea and bread. He was not going home as he told me he was. Noel insisted he was attending school, and we thought perhaps he was attending sometimes, but we knew he was not going regularly. Joan knew Noel's blind grandmother and his mother; obviously, they were not looking after their children. We found out where they were staying and went for a visit one day. The whole family lived in two little rooms. We also found out where Noel went to school and stopped by to talk with the headmaster. He told us Noel was a brilliant child, but he was coming to class only once or twice a week and was not going to pass into the next grade under those circumstances. Since Joan had already talked with Noel many times about this, I took him aside the next day and spoke to him. I said, "Noel, we love you, and we want to help you. We know you love Jesus Christ. You are a precious child, and God has gifted you in many ways. But if you don't stay in school, we're not going to be able to work with you and see you reach your potential. You won't know how to read and write as well as you should, and you won't be able to grow up to be a leader."

Timothy Masungu was another kid with whom we spent Christmas. He came onto the streets after the death of his mother, probably from HIV-AIDS. His father had remarried, and the new wife didn't want Timothy to live with them. When Joan and I visited his father's home, it was sad to hear his stepmother degrade Timothy. He was a smart young boy who had had to drop out of school. He told me he knew he needed to go back to school or he would be in trouble in the future. He wanted a library card so he could read books. Eventually we made all the arrangements to enroll him in a local primary school and bought him school uniforms. Helping him get the shirt, shorts, hat, tie, shoes, and knee socks was an experience that Timothy and I both enjoyed. He told the sales people I was his "auntie." He attended classes for about six to eight weeks, but then he dropped out of school. Several of us tried to talk to him, but by then he was addicted to glue and to life on the streets. He went back to living on the streets, begging, sniffing glue, and struggling daily to survive. He kept calling me "auntie" and stayed in touch for a time, but it was very painful to see what happened to him. He would come sometimes for tea and bread from Joan. When Joan or I saw him, we prayed for him and told him that Jesus loved him, and we loved him also. We prayed for a better life for him, but it was heartbreaking to find him stoned a lot of the time from sniffing glue or using other drugs.

Innocent Mudzonga, another boy we befriended around this time, had been on the streets for two years. During this time, he hadn't gone to school. His stepfather drank too much and hit Innocent's mother. Unfortunately, his mother often told lies, and Innocent himself became adept at twisting the truth. Sometimes Innocent was beaten by his parents. He wanted to return to school and, with the help of the Social Welfare Department, Joan and I were able to find a distant relative who would allow him to live with her and attend seventh grade. Bill and I helped him with school uniforms, shoes, and other needs. His adopted family was happy to have him in their home, and they said he was not a problem for them. He was honored for his achievement in school, and he vowed he would never return to the streets to live.

Two years later Innocent was able to attend Mhondoro Secondary School, a boarding school run by the Presbyterian Church of Zimbabwe. At that time, Rev. Paul Neshangwe was chaplain at this school and helped get a scholarship for Innocent. Paul and his wife, Lydia, took a keen interest in Innocent and worked with him. Innocent did well during the four years at Mhondoro. However, after he finished secondary school, he found himself back on the streets with some of his old friends. The pull of the streets is so strong! It is like an addictive drug. Right before Bill and I left Harare in November 2001, I found Innocent one morning near the grocery store where I shopped. He had been drinking beer even though it was only 10:00 a.m. I asked him if he had eaten anything and he said he had not, so we went upstairs to a restaurant to get him some sadza with meat and greens. He poured out his heart to me, cried and told me he had returned to street life. He said he knew he had let Pastor Neshangwe and me down. I told him he had really let himself down. I prayed with him and talked to him about his future. I asked him if I could call Rev. Neshangwe and see if he could help him find a job. He agreed. I did call Paul, but Innocent didn't go to see him. About a year later, after Bill and I were living in Orlando, Innocent called me from Cape Town, South Africa, where he said he was working. He still phones me from time to time to let me know where he is. I tell him that I pray that he is well and following Jesus. He says he is still attending church and reading his Bible.

There were other caring adults who played significant roles in the lives of many of the young kids. Soon after Maury and I began working together, we met Annie Sinclair, a beautiful, committed Christian young woman from the U.K. She had been doing artwork with the kids in Harare Gardens. She said she'd like to get in on the weekly meetings we were having in the park with the kids. Annie was a pretty, blue-eyed blonde and may have looked frail to some, but underneath she was made of steel. Annie was a gifted artist, but more than that, she had such a heart for the kids from the streets and for all children who are poor and needy. She had given herself totally to the Lord to use all her talents and abilities to help others to build up God's Kingdom there. She was a great addition to our team. With her friend Caroline, Annie took over the art, Maury did drama and games, and I continued the Bible study.

Since we could not come up with another place to get together, we continued meeting in the park. Noel was always there, and he brought along several other children with whom we continued to work. However, we came to realize fairly quickly that the park was not a safe place. The young girls who had joined us were getting hit on, and there were always thieves nearby.

Bill was very supportive. Often when we went to the park to be with the kids, he went too and sat at a little distance, working on reports or financial records. Bill traveled considerably more than I did because, as I got more and more involved with the kids, I chose to stay behind to work with Maury, Joan, and Annie. The three of us often got together at our flat to pray and think about what we could do for these children. Finally, it came to us. We decided to ask City Presbyterian Church, located in downtown Harare, if we could use their beautiful, spacious fellowship hall once a week to meet with the kids. We wanted to play games, tell Bible stories, give them some food and have some interaction with them away from the streets. We wanted to have more time to spend with them. Most of this plan was Joan's idea, but the group decided I should be the one to ask the pastor and session of City Presbyterian for permission, because Bill and I, as Presbyterian missionaries, already had a relationship with the pastor and some members of the congregation. So, I approached the pastor to ask if we could use the fellowship hall. Because Presbyterians have to do things "decently and in order," the pastor asked us to write a letter stating what we wanted to do. Bill and I wrote that we wanted to work with some vulnerable children (we didn't call them street kids), to open the church doors and invite them in, feed them, and talk with them about the love of Jesus Christ. We wanted to hear from the children, let them share their concerns with us, and play games together. The session agreed, and we started making plans to begin this ministry.

Annie, Caroline, and others continued to work with us for a while, but Maury had returned to the U.S. shortly after Christmas to finish college. Then Caroline left, and Annie returned to the U.K to get her Master's degree in art, but said she planned to come back to Zimbabwe afterwards.

In April 1995, we began meeting at City Presbyterian Church on Wednesday evenings from 5:00 to 7:00. Volunteers from several Presbyterian congregations nearby came to help with this out-reach program. Fifteen children showed up for our first meeting at City Church. By that summer, we were feeding ninety kids at our Wednesday night meetings. I helped get things organized on Wednesday afternoons. I boiled eggs, *hundreds* of eggs,— until I thought I never wanted to boil another egg! —while others made peanut butter sandwiches. We'd give the kids a sandwich, an egg, juice, usually a piece of fruit such as a banana or an orange, and maybe a "sweet" as they called a piece of candy. We wanted to give them milk, but it was just too expensive. We started out doing what we could. As word got around, we began to receive help from several other Presbyterian churches. A couple of pastors helped, as well as Bill when he was in town. By that time, Rev. Don Fauchelle a New Zealander, was the interim pastor at City Presbyterian. He and his wife, Margaret, were great supporters of this Wednesday evening program. Don would sometimes read or tell a Bible story. The kids loved having him around.

Our son Shamba came for a three-month visit in March 1995 and was a tremendous help with the kids—playing ball, getting to know them, and helping us with Wednesday activities. Joan and Shamba became very close. Shamba would get up early in the morning to help her serve tea and bread. When she needed to take a child to the hospital, he would often ride with her. Joan called him her oth-er son. It was so special for us that Shamba could be with us as we began our ministry with these kids. We also enjoyed our son William's visit that summer with his fiancé Kathryn Miller. In December, we returned home to attend their wedding on December 9th and to spend Christmas with our family. We stayed for two months more to speak in churches. During this time, my sister Peggy was diagnosed with terminal cancer. I was grateful to be able to spend some time with her before we left the States. Her death in August was a shock to us all.

Though it was difficult to return to Harare in February 1996, we were committed to continuing the Wednesday night meetings with the vulnerable children. It's not difficult to imagine the problems we had in bringing ninety children from the streets to have a program in the fellowship hall of a downtown church! We had to check them to make sure they didn't have cigarettes, alcohol or glue, because the church leaders had asked us to make sure they didn't bring those substances inside the hall. Many children on the streets sniffed glue that they kept in baby food jars or plastic bags. They'd put a little spoonful of glue in the bag and sniff it to get high. We had several Zimbabwean pastors and young elders who were willing to help as volunteers to interact with the kids, and to check their pockets to make sure they didn't bring forbidden items into the hall. A large garbage bag was kept at the door for anything that was confiscated. The kids had to relinquish the banned substances if they wanted to come in. We were amazed they were so willing to do this in order to have a meal and some fellowship.

As we worked with the children, I was often reminded of the passage in John 21:15–17 where Jesus asked Peter, "Do you love me?" and then said, "Feed my sheep." We found that there were plenty of "sheep" to be fed and both little and big "lambs" to be tended in Zimbabwe. Ann Weems' thought-provoking poem, "Feeding Sheep,"[iv] was an inspiration to me and seemed very applicable to our situation:

He said, "Feed my sheep."

There were no conditions:

Least of all, Feed my sheep if they deserve it.

Feed my sheep if you have any leftovers.

Feed my sheep if the mood strikes you.

If the economy's OK …

If you're not too busy …

No conditions… just, "Feed my sheep."

Could it be that God's Kingdom will come when each lamb is fed?

We who have agreed to keep covenant are called to feed sheep

Even when it means the grazing will be done on our own front lawns.

Maury Mendenhall compiled drawings and words of some of the street children and called it *Tichaona* ("We Will See"). Here are a few examples of what the children had to say:

- "Sometimes bad parents beat up their children." (Innocent, age 11)

- "Bad parents tell their children to go to town to find money." (Innocent, age 13)

- "Bad parents usually dump their children, some in toilets, some just leave the child without shelter. I think some people sniff glue so they will not feel cold. Some smoke glue so they can get money and so they can sleep and forget their problems." (Sylas, age 12)

- "I'm sorry to be a street kid, because sometimes I take food from the [rubbish] bin. When I am sleeping on the sidewalk, people they come and walk on top of me. And sometimes animals attack you. Like a dog. It can attack you. And thieves, they can attack you also." (Timothy, age 13)

- "The police they hate us. If they catch you they are going to beat you and hit you and at the jail they are going to treat us like hell, like prisoners." (Innocent, age 11)

- "It is too better to sleep in a drain just because in a drain there is not much cold but if you always sleep in the drainage you will not have enough oxygen and if someone takes a cardboard and makes it burn all the smoke will attack you and you will not have enough air." (Innocent, age 13)

- "People can buy me bread and clothes but that is not enough. I think more than anything I want to go to school." (Obert, age 13)

- "There is nothing I like about being a street kid. Everything is so bad. For me when I am dirty I will be shy to move around town because if I meet someone I know I sometimes run away from him because people think I can not care for myself—that I am lazy and sick. And I will be shy." (Neville, age 13)

- "If you've got nice clothes other people can love you. If you don't have nice clothes your other friend can say he can't play with you because "you are dirty. So I don't want to walk with you." When people say things like that you have to walk by yourself and you start to think, I am not a person." (Farai, age 15)

Noel was one of the kids who came to the Wednesday evening program, although he did not participate as much as the kids who did not have a place to stay. Joan felt we probably needed to encourage Noel to go home before dark each evening so that he would be ready for school. He lived about a thirty- or forty-minute bus ride from Harare so we gave him bus fare. We got to know the headmaster of his school very well. In fact, I had his phone number and would call periodically to see if Noel had been in school that week. We'd try to give Noel a reward if he had been attending class. Noel had a younger brother, Tendai, who was only about seven years old. We began helping Tendai also, as Noel felt responsible for his brother, giving both boys bus money to go home at night.

Bill was a great help to us as we as we got started on our Wednesday evening program. It was chaotic at first when we had sixty, eighty, and then ninety kids who were not used to standing in a line. Some older teenagers would try to get two or three plates and push the little ones aside. I'm pretty good with faces and I could usually tell who had already been through the line, but with Bill's help we did get more organized. We bought plastic plates and cups with Presbyterian gifts and with The Outreach Foundation funds. Bill suggested that we number the plates and cups from one to ninety. That was the "ticket" each child had to have coming through the line. They were so hungry that at first, we fed them as soon as they arrived, but then we figured out that some of the kids slipped out before our Bible study and prayer time. We wanted to interact and talk with them about Jesus Christ, not just give them food. This was important—spiritual nourishment, to share with them about Jesus' love for them, and our love for them. Pretty soon, though, we realized we needed to play a game when they first arrived in order to work off some of their energy, although we tried to manage the activity level so as not to break windows and such. I have fond memories of Ball in the Hall. Several younger pastors and volunteers including Rev. Paul Neshangwe played with the kids and became an important part of this program. After the games, we had a Bible study and after that, the food. We discovered that after they had eaten, they were a little more willing to open up and talk about their problems. In fact, we were surprised that the children were as frank as they were. This was in 1995, and they were talking openly about sexual abuse and HIV-AIDS, a subject that was almost taboo at that time in the Shona culture.

A young Presbyterian doctor from the U.S., Anne Peterson, also helped at the program. Her husband, Dan Peterson, was teaching at the University Medical School in Harare. Both Anne and Dan were doctors, but Anne was not allowed to work because the Zimbabwe government would not give her a work permit. Through Highland Presbyterian, the church she was attending in Harare, she heard that we were feeding kids. Once we got to know each other, she offered to come and talk to the children about keeping healthy. Her input was especially important since many of the problems the kids shared were related to health. For example, they didn't have access to clean water and were eating spoiled food out of garbage cans. With Anne's help, we added a health lesson. Anne planned and shared health tips with the kids and talked openly and honestly about HIV-AIDS. Unfortunately, sexual abuse was a reality in the lives of kids who had been on the streets for very long. It was tough to hear what they had to say. We would then ask how we could pray for them and were amazed how many of them—particularly the little ones—wanted to get off the streets right away, because they were afraid at night, sleeping under the streets in drains or gutters. Many of them kept saying they wanted to go back to school.

Dr. Peterson contributed a chapter to *The Hope Factor*.[v] In it, she wrote of her experiences in Harare:

> *The AIDS epidemic in southern Africa began almost a decade later than the East African epidemic, but it surged much more quickly. By 1994 when we arrived in Harare, the epidemic was already maturing. One of the saddest consequences of this was the growing orphan problem. The streets of Harare had hundreds of street children, some of whom had family to go home to at night, but many others who had no place to go. I began to take bread when I went downtown so that I would have some appropriate way to respond to the begging. But I realized it wasn't enough.*
>
> *Nancy Warlick, an energetic Presbyterian activist who had lived for years in Kinshasa, Zaire, helped me learn and serve in an additional way. Her friend, Joan, known as the Bread Lady, would bring bread every day to about 50 street children. Nancy and Joan gathered a group to have a weekly Wednesday night outreach to the street children at City Presbyterian Church. Nearly one hundred children, ages 6–19, would come. (They were almost all boys because it was dangerous for girls to be on the streets.) Many had either biblical or character-based names such as Ezekiel or Innocent.*
>
> *The central activity was dinner, preceded by game time and followed by a lesson. Occasionally I would bring my own children, now in grade school, to play soccer in the church gym*

with the street children. During the lesson time, the littlest ones would sit on our laps, happy to have someone, even a stranger, hold and care for them even for a few minutes.

Initially, I provided medical care to those who needed it, usually between 5 and 10 patients a week. My hope was to build a relationship with the kids so that eventually I could talk to them about their risk for AIDS. The major medical problems that I saw, diarrhea and pneumonia, were hygiene-related. A month or so into our weekly visits, I prepared to lead a discussion on "How to stay healthy while living on the streets." (We had already instituted hand-washing prior to eating as part of the dinner routine. I was content that there were some small things that we and they could do to respond to the challenges of daily life on the street.)

I hoped that in a few weeks, we could talk about AIDS. So, I was astounded when they told me right off the bat that their biggest problems were hunger, diarrhea, sexually transmitted diseases (STDs), AIDS, and having to sell themselves to get food. These were brave boys, admitting to homosexual prostitution in Africa, where this is a hidden and forbidden topic. In that very first lesson, they were ready to learn about AIDS and discuss ways to change their lives and, if possible, to reduce their exposure to AIDS.

A college student who was doing a summer internship asked them about their lives before they lived in the streets, what it was like now, and what their hopes and dreams were. They said they wanted to have families, go back to school, and be warm and safe. With all they endured, they yearned for normal lives.

The Success School

Joan was instrumental during these Wednesday nights. She was familiar with all the kids, knew their stories, and knew some of their parents or relatives. The adult leaders had meetings and prayed together about what we were doing. At one meeting in our living room, we particularly felt God's presence when we talked about starting some kind of basic remedial school that would help the kids get ready to go back into the mainstream government schools. Many kids told us over and over again that they wanted to go to school but didn't have the chance to go. Most of them would be up all night and would sleep during the day. Some didn't have the resources, such as a watch, to let them know it was time for school to start. Others had no adult encouragement or lacked the commitment or discipline to return to school. Several children without a good place to stay were sleeping under the streets in a drain area, and it's pretty hard to get up and go to school from that situation.

We decided we would again go to City Presbyterian Church to ask if we could start a school on their property. They agreed to our request and offered us a large room upstairs over the sanctuary. By that time, we had met Mrs. Alice Chikomo, a retired schoolteacher and a member at City Church. Her husband, Herbert Chikomo, was a pastor on staff at the church. Alice, Joan, Margaret Fauchelle, and I were the four who started the school. Joan was still giving out tea and bread in the mornings and talked to the kids about coming to the school at City Church. We wound up with thirty or forty students who were seriously interested in attending classes three days a week at the church.

We were always amazed that God provided incredible volunteers to come help us. This shouldn't have been such a surprise, because we knew God had arranged it all beforehand. Jesus said the children were to be brought to Him to be blessed and cared for. We were merely fleshing out His love. One of the school volunteers was an American lady, a PhD who taught reading classes for teachers at UCLA, and she brought some other teachers to help. She was an expert, and God knew we needed her! Helping with our school, she said later, was one of the most fulfilling projects she'd ever been involved in. She planned to stay in Harare through the summer and said she would give us six weeks of her time and expertise. As the students came in, she determined each child's reading level and made suggestions on placement. She explained that reading was the best indicator for putting the children in groups. I loved the name she gave our school, The Success School. We were helping these kids prepare for getting back into a regular school and for future success in life.

We had three or four teachers at the beginning. Alice taught, but also was the director of the school. I enjoyed teaching but because Bill and I traveled, I could not commit to being regular staff three days every week. However, I loved being with these special kids, encouraging them, teaching them, and getting to know them. Bill and I promised to be sure the school always had money for eggs, peanut butter sandwiches, weak tea with milk and sugar, and fruit. When I was there, I taught some and served as a resource person. I became the physical education teacher and during the morning recess, I led the kids in games or exercises. This was such a fun time. They relished doing jumping jacks or stretches and playing games that everyone could participate in, like Drop the Hanky or The Hokey Pokey.

The school met from 8:00 to 11:00 in the morning; then the children were fed a snack. The thing that amazed us most was that these children would actually get up and out of the streets in the morning and get there on time. Joan and I didn't feel punctuality should be such a rigid rule, and yet we were the ones asked to talk to the kids who were late. I still have pictures in my mind of these dear kids lined up on the church sidewalk before 8:00 waiting for school to begin, dressed in their rags but with smiling, happy faces, eager to learn. Since this was a downtown church, the gates were locked at night and it was necessary to have security measures. The children had to wait each morning for the church gates to be opened. More than once, tears welled up as I came down the street and saw thirty or so "rag tag" students waiting quietly and patiently in line for school to start.

On the nights we had our Wednesday meetings, we got permission for the children to shower next door at a community pool. People at the pool didn't want the children to go swimming, because they were so dirty. We were responsible for giving them soap and towels, and we agreed that we wouldn't let them get into trouble or bring in glue or cigarettes. The boys would only shower and put on clean clothes, all under adult supervision, and then come to the meetings. Later, we made the same proposal for The Success School, so the children were allowed shower each day before class.

Most of the children were in rags when we first met them. We would give them clothing and shoes on Wednesday nights, especially when it was cold, but the clothes we handed out would be stolen, particularly from the young ones. Margaret Fauchelle hit upon the idea that it would be good to let the children have school uniforms. The kids were *very* interested in that, so we went downtown to purchase khaki shorts and shirts on sale at Woolworth's. The manager gave us a big discount when he heard what we were doing. We knew that if the students took the uniforms out the door and into the streets, the clothes would get dirty or be stolen. So instead we gave them each a plastic grocery bag that included a little bit of soap for their shower. The shower was outdoors so several children could shower at the same time. Those who came to school would come into a changing area where they could put on their school uniforms. We watched them go from dirty rags to actually looking like other children who went to school. While in class at City Church, they would sit in their uniforms and they were *so* proud—even if they had no shoes or just old flip-flops. We found their behavior improved when they were wearing uniforms. Several of the stores began giving us leftover uniforms, or we would purchase a certain number and they would add some extras. We were very touched. On many occasions, local people brought us food. Highland Presbyterian Church in Harare had already been helping Joan. When they found out we were running the school, the church wanted to give the school a donation for food as well.

We had lots of Zimbabwean volunteers, and I laugh as I remember one of the visiting pastors who said to me that it was hard to tell the volunteers from the street kids, because some of the volunteers looked pretty ragged. But these volunteers were Christians who had heard about the program and wanted to come and help. One dear lady came from a Presbyterian church in a poor area. Although she didn't have much herself, she wanted to help. Her parents had died when she was a child, probably of AIDS, so she related to the plight of these kids. She was married and pregnant but left her family to take the forty-five-minute bus ride each Wednesday evening to come and help. She didn't speak much English, but she prayed with us and helped make peanut butter sandwiches. She volunteered for several weeks until it began to get dark during our preparation time. She didn't want to be out after dark and her baby was due, so finally she felt it was time to stop coming. I thanked God for her and her desire to help these children. I know that God was using this ministry with children to touch all of us, to change our lives, and to widen the circle of people who could be involved. We all knew that "even the least of these" street kids were God's children; God loved them and wanted them to be taken care of. All of us learned so much together while helping these children.

Many of the children needed medical attention. Joan wound up taking on this responsibility. Some children suffering from a bad case of malaria would need to go to a hospital, and others would get cut while rough housing when they were sniffing glue. There was a clinic nearby run by Catholic nuns whom Joan already knew. Often the children would be treated free of charge there. If kids arrived at school sick, coughing or injured, Joan would take them to the clinic to be checked. We provided cough medicine, aspirin and other simple helps like vitamins and throat lozenges that the children could not afford on their own.

Annie Sinclair came back from the U.K. in late 1995. It was obvious that some of the children had a great deal of talent, and that was why she had wanted a Master's degree, to learn more about how to work with them. Bill suggested that she find another Presbyterian church where she and her friend Caroline could work with some of the older boys who were really gifted. Bill talked with Pastor Jonah Masaka out in Kwadzana, one of the high-density areas. His church had quite an impressive outreach to women's groups for sewing and Bible study, to men and teenagers being trained as welders, and other outreach programs. So, Annie's group, known first as "Madi Zimbabwe" and later as "New Creations," began to meet there. They set up tables outside where they could paint and work freely. They began creating lovely batiks. Annie had a recipe for paint using flour and water, and she was quite creative with the batik designs. They also made cards, wire animals, and other projects that were fairly successful fund-raisers. Some of the items were sent to the U.K. to be sold, and groups coming from the U.S bought others. I was dubbed a "patron of the arts" because Bill and I would take some of the beautiful batiks back to the U.S. to be sold. Annie usually took the older boys into her program. They were the harder ones to help; they had been on the street longer, and their bad habits were more ingrained and difficult to break. Annie often asked Pastor Jonah to speak to the boys, teach them some life skills and help them to turn away from the things that were dragging them down. The pastor would do Bible studies with them and help them turn toward Jesus Christ, so they could indeed become new creations in Christ.

Annie felt that John Moyo was one of the most artistically talented young men she had ever worked with. He was also the first of Annie's group to be baptized by Pastor Jonah. John had started out at our program at City Church on Wednesday nights. At first, I didn't notice him because he was so quiet, but when I asked him when he had accepted Jesus Christ he said, "You know, Nancy, at the programs. You told us about Jesus, that He loves us." When John

John Moyo showing the beautiful batik that he made

was baptized, Bill and I were gone, but many of the people who worked with us were there. I thought about how God works, even when we have no idea how God is using us—working in the hearts of these kids, changing their hearts and minds, making them new creations in Christ. John got into a church Bible study and really worked on doing what God wanted him to do. He had a great influence on some of the other young men. We found out later that John's name was actually Pedro.

Pedro had fled his home at the age of eight during the raging civil war in Mozambique. He came to Harare and lived and worked on the streets for eleven years. Pedro was one of the young men who helped me understand how lonely street children are. "Nancy," he explained, "it's so easy to go along with anybody who shows you any attention or concern … you know, the drinking and smoking and all that. I'm not strong. I followed along behind the leaders in our group. It's hard for me to stand up against them. I'm the only one among my friends to stop drinking and smoking. Please pray for me." He saw himself as a follower and not a leader. "Pedro," I told him, "you have been strong because you have endured to this point. You were one of the first to go to church, to attend Bible study and then be baptized."

Pedro became an outstanding artist. He once asked me for photos of giraffes because he wanted to put them in the batik scenes he was making. I still have some of his beautiful batiks. One with three giraffes hangs in our living room today.

Bill and I had the joy and distinct privilege of locating Pedro's stepfather in Maputo, Mozambique, in 1997 and telling him about his son, whom he thought was dead. This story is much like the prodigal son in Luke 15. Pedro's mother and stepfather came to Harare to see him and to visit us and thank us for reuniting them. We kept telling his family what a gifted young man he was and what a fine Christian. After his stepfather saw Pedro in Harare, he admitted that he himself had backslid and had not been going to church. He said to us, "My son is probably a better Christian than I am."

Pedro ended up going back to Mozambique to join his family.

Annie helped him arrange the trip, and we gave him money to get a passport right before Bill and I left Zimbabwe in 2001. I'm not sure if he ever came back to Harare. He was twenty-five years old when he left, a grown man. This was one of those special situations in which we could help one of our kids, a youngster whom we had come to know and love, connect with his family and return home. (We called them *our* kids but, of course, they are all God's kids.) Pedro is one of those extraordinary young men that I think about, wondering where he is living now and how he is doing.

A few years later, Annie left Rev. Jonah's church, because the program outgrew the facilities there. She had a vision for wanting the older boys to learn to grow crops and become self-sustaining. River of Life, a church on the other side of town, took them in. They had some houses where the young men could live and property where they could raise their food. The people of the church really ministered to these young men, not just a few times a week at Bible study, but every morning. They prayed with them, and Annie diligently worked with them and cared for them.

Another of the young men Annie helped was named Simba, thin and tall, maybe six-feet, two-inches, with dreadlocks. He told us he was younger than he actually was in order to get into our program. Simba loved to do drama and enjoyed coming to our meetings. You could see the pull between good and evil, between the devil and the Lord in his life. Eventually he did not stick with our program, because he was making money "pimping" some of the younger children on the streets. It broke my heart when I realized all of this.

Freedom was one of the most talented boys we ever worked with, a good-looking young man, gifted in art and drama. He had gone only through the eighth grade in school but spoke English well. Freedom worked for a time with us and with Annie, but he lacked discipline and was another one who was not able to overcome the pull of the streets. Interestingly though, he said he was a Christian. His grandfather had taken him to church. He knew many of the Bible stories and could tell them to the younger ones. We tried to get him to go back to school, but he refused. I met for a time with him to read the Bible, pray and talk together. He liked the Gospel of John. Annie and I got a job for Freedom and Simba to be in a film, "Everyone's Child," about kids from the streets directed by Tsitsi Dangarembga, the first black Zimbabwean woman to direct a feature film. Freedom and Simba were to be paid for their part in the film by the producer, who was from the U.K. Bill agreed to be the "bank" to hold the funds for them. I suggested that Freedom use some of the money he earned to take art lessons or drama lessons: "You are at a crossroad in your life. One road you can take would be a good path, the path that allows you to get some kind of skill and make you feel fulfilled. The other path is the wrong one for you. I'm concerned that if you take that wrong path and waste this money, it will lead to your destruction." We talked about this quite a bit. He told me how much his grandfather had meant to him when he used to talk to him, read Scripture to him, and take him to church.

There was a lot of excitement as the film was being made. Although not Christian, it was a good film. At the end of the movie, we asked the director and producer to give the money to Simba and Freedom in our presence, so we could be there to encourage them to use it wisely. But the next day Annie came to tell us that the boys were given the money, about $2000 each, without our being there. Freedom came to Bill the next day with about $500 and asked him to keep it for him. Bill asked him where the rest of the money was; we realized that a lot of it had already been spent. Bill had Freedom's money for four or five days, and then Freedom came by about nine o'clock one night and asked for his money. I told him Bill was not awake and even banks had certain hours; he would have to wait until the next day. He was back again the next day asking for all of his money. He was 18 or 19 by then and had earned the money, so there was nothing Bill could do but give it to him. I think he and Simba had had quite a party and treated their friends to whatever they wanted for several days. I had been aware for some time that we were losing both of these young men. Increasingly, I saw Freedom drunk and heard stories about the things he was doing. He quit meeting us at church. He came to say goodbye when we left Zimbabwe in 2001, but I think he was probably drunk at the time. I was very disheartened, but I remember praying for him. I told him he could still change and that Jesus Christ still loved him and wanted to be his Savior. Sadly, on one of our trips back in 2002, I heard that he had been hit and killed by a car as he was walking drunk in the middle of the road downtown. I hope he is in heaven. I know Freedom meant even more to Jesus Christ than he did to those of us who worked with him. He was a precious young man; one we won't forget.

Annie suffered many hardships. She was hit over the head and her passport stolen; several times she was followed by young men who were attracted by her beauty and seeming frailty, but she was never daunted. She loved the Lord and knew she was called to work with these young men. Sometimes she spent the night at our apartment when she was unable to go home safely. Finally in 2006, she found that she was on a government "list." She had become engaged to a Zimbabwean and did not want to leave the country, but being young and vulnerable, as well as a citizen of the U.K., made her a person at risk. When she had trouble getting her visa renewed, she finally left the country and went back to the U.K. She married her Zimbabwean fiancé there. They had a daughter and now have a second child. She and her husband would love to go back and work in Zimbabwe, but at this point her husband is studying, and they will stay put while the political situation remains bad in Zimbabwe.

Melfort Farm

During the time Annie was working with the older boys, those of us helping at City Presbyterian continued to have school three mornings a week. By early summer 1996, we realized that many of the kids who were coming to school regularly from the streets were showing us that they genuinely did want to change their lifestyle. Most of them proclaimed that they loved Jesus Christ. We began to pray about the next phase that God would have us be involved in. There was a farm about thirteen miles from Harare out in the Melfort area. The women of the Zanu-PF Party, President Mugabe's political party, owned it. (Actually Zanu-PF was considered by Mugabe and his followers to be the *only* political party.) We learned that these women were interested in helping some "street kids" be relocated, so we met with their leaders and received approval to relocate some of our children to the farm. There was a primary school and dining hall, a dorm, and even beds. We never thought of Melfort as a permanent place for children, but we thought it could help them get away from the dangers and temptations of the downtown area of the capital city, at least through their primary years.

In December 1996, we helped to relocate about forty children. At that time, Joan was driving a car that didn't always start. Bill and I had our four-wheel-drive Nissan Patrol. I don't remember exactly how many trips we made to transport kids to the farm that first day. First, we took the boys who really wanted to make a move and were ready to go. We hoped they would get permission from their families if they had an available family member, but we decided to let this responsibility be on the kids. Those who wanted to live at the farm needed to agree that they would stay there and go to school regularly. The farm would help provide a safe place for the boys and the opportunity to go to the primary school; they would have food to eat, clothing to wear, and would be able to live this phase of their lives as students. We maintained a presence for four or five years at Melfort Farm. Gifts of food and money poured in. God blessed and multiplied the funds that came from PC(USA) members and congregations, much of it given through The Outreach Foundation. We also received gifts of money, clothing, and food from local people and from Presbyterian congregations, like Highland Presbyterian Church in Harare.

Xavier was one of the boys Joan and I felt was special. He must have been eight or nine years old at the time. He had been coming on Wednesday nights and obviously had sniffed glue a lot. Often the kids would have glue on their clothing or on their faces, so it was easy to know what they were doing. Xavier had such a precious face. He had attended school at City Presbyterian and had progressed with his reading and math skills. His behavior improved and he began to have a more joyful outlook. However, for several weeks prior to our going to Melfort, Xavier had been sleeping in the drains under the street. He had been high on glue one evening when he lay down to sleep. He pulled some old cardboard boxes over himself for cover. An older boy threw kerosene on the cardboard, then lit a match and threw it on the boxes covering Xavier. He was badly burned. The next morning when he came to get tea and bread, Joan saw the burns on his neck and back and immediately took him to the hospital. The hospital personnel said he had to have extensive treatment. Joan took him daily to have his burns treated and cleaned. She was so loving and caring. I really believe it was sometime during that period, when he saw that Joan was willing to take him to the hospital and care for him, that he felt he was worth something. The burns were serious, and for several weeks we worried about infection. But we prayed over him, and God's wonderful healing mercies prevailed. Joan was the angel God used. It was incredible that Xavier had no serious scars from the burns, but I know that experience was a defining one for him. Driving out to the farm in my car, I could tell he was excited, even though he was rather quiet.

Sometime after Xavier and the other boys arrived at Melfort, Pam Kidd, a writer and Presbyterian pastor's wife, came from the U.S. with her husband, David, to do a story on street kids in Harare. I had written Pam, asking her to come. When she agreed, I helped organize her visit and got permission for her to come to Melfort to interview the boys. Xavier was not one of the children chosen to sit with Pam and tell her his story. While Pam was interviewing other kids, Xavier kept following me around and saying, "Nancy, I want to tell my story; I want to share." So, I asked David to sit with us under a tree. It was a chilly July day, and I remember that Xavier had holes in his shirt and no shoes on his feet. Unfortunately, bad habits persisted at the farm. We had given sweaters and shoes to all the children, but evidently Xavier's had been stolen. I told him I knew he was cold and asked if he wanted to go inside, but he said no, we could sit under the tree.

Xavier started the interview by saying, "Nancy, isn't God wonderful!" I just about lost it. I said, "Yes, Xavier, God *is* wonderful," but I looked away so he couldn't see my tears. This boy—with no shoes, holes in his shirt, and a family situation that was a mess—was telling me joyfully that God is wonderful.

He shared what God had done in his life. I was amazed at how he had gone from a young boy living on the streets, sniffing glue, sleeping in gutters, to this teenager going to school and doing well. He continued telling us how God had blessed him by allowing him to come to the farm and go to school. On Sundays he was attending a nearby Pentecostal church, a congregation with a kind pastor who preached the Word of God. Xavier said he knew God loved him. As he poured out his heart, I realized this was a boy who had truly been touched and changed by God. All I could say through my tears was, "Yes, yes, God is wonderful." I looked over and saw that David Kidd also had tears in his eyes. We were both looking away because we did not want Xavier to see what an emotional moment this was for us. It was a special confirming time when God let me see that He had more in store for these children than we even imagined. I realized that if we obeyed Jesus' command to bring the children to Him, God's love would transform them!

Tichaona, another boy at Melfort, wanted to be called John Ali, a name he gave himself when he went onto the streets. His father died in January 1995 but had divorced his mother several years before. John was a very confused boy. I don't know if his mother had put him out of the home or if she had already died, but at an early age, probably eight or nine, he went to live on the streets. We learned later that he had an aunt and a sister in the Melfort area. He was not always cooperative and would often vent his anger by lashing out at the other boys. Joan had known him for some time, but I first met him when we began our program at City Presbyterian Church. John Ali decided that he wanted to come to our school. He was about ten or eleven years old when we met him, quite large for his age, and belligerent. He sniffed glue, beat up the other children, and was a "hard nut to crack." We did agree to have him in our school and allowed him to come to our meetings, but we really had to watch him. At times we had to tell him he could not stay in school for the rest of the day, because he had tried to hurt one of the other kids. But we would pray for him. Joan and I particularly tried to reach out to him.

Then John Ali developed a new problem. He had a growth of some sort under his knee. He cried in pain, unusual behavior for him because he was a macho sort of guy. Joan decided to do something about it. She took him to a hospital. The doctors felt he needed to be kept at the hospital and put in traction for six weeks. While he was there, Joan and I brought him food, and we left money with the nurses to help him get what he needed. His sister and a couple of family members got word and came to visit him, but they didn't come for regular visits. It was obvious that he was dealing with a lot of anger. We tried to talk with his sister about his situation but didn't get much information from her about her brother's life. She did say there wasn't room for him to live with her.

We found out that John Ali and I shared the same birthday, November 15. He was still in the hospital on that day, so Joan and I took him a birthday cake and had a party. He loved that we celebrated our birthdays together with Joan. After that, we saw a real change in him. He laughed with us and thanked us for coming. Joan brought a game that we played with him. I brought him a Bible and several other books to read. He often looked at Joan and me and seemed to be wondering, "Why are you doing this for me? Why do you care about me?" We kept encouraging him: "John, you are important! We love you." He started reading the Bible every day while he was in the hospital. We had been worried that John had cancer, and we talked about that possibility with him. We were greatly relieved when the doctors said that the growth wasn't malignant.

We knew by then that his real name was Tichaona, so we asked him which name he wanted to be called. He admitted he had taken John Ali as a macho name—often the kids on the streets did that. He told us he'd like to be called Tichaona. I'd given him a small Bible earlier, but the Bible I brought on his birthday was a special one. We also brought him some sweets. He started crying one day and told us he wanted to thank us. He said he wanted to change his life. We prayed for him and thanked God for this special time with him. We were so pleased for the change we were beginning to see in him.

The following month we were moving the kids out of town to the farm. Tichaona's sister lived in a little town between Harare and Melfort Farm. All we knew was what Tichaona had told us: that his mother didn't like him and had left. Obviously, he was still bitter and continuing to deal with a lot of unfortunate things that had happened to him. The hospital staff said in order to heal he needed to eat regularly, take care of himself, and not hang around the streets. We took him from the hospital and went to where his sister stayed. I told her there was a possibility that he could move to the farm at Melfort soon, where there were dormitories and a primary school, but she was hesitant to take him even for a brief time because she had only one room. She was about twenty years old, and he was thirteen by then. She said if she did allow him to stay, she couldn't keep him very long. She really didn't want to take responsibility for him, but she finally agreed to help him until he could move to Melfort Farm. When the day came for me to pick him up in my car, we sent word for him to come to the road to meet me. He was there with one small suitcase in his hand. He was smiling, actually beaming. Thankfully, he did not cause problems at the farm. Jesus really had made a difference in his life. That day in the hospital when he told us he wanted to change, he said, "I know Jesus is my Savior and I know I have not been nice to the other boys on the street, particularly the little ones. I want to change." And he did change. He even told us he wanted to be a pastor. How special it was to see the love of Jesus transform Tichaona's life.

When Tichaona arrived at Melfort Farm, we learned that he loved to garden. He really could make things grow and would work for hours in the garden. We brought seeds for him. Gardening was a great idea, because the kids could raise some of the vegetables they needed in their diet. They loved greens and a relish of tomatoes and onions with their sadza, the staple dish made from cooked corn flour and water. But the director at Melfort thought the vegetables belonged to her, so we would often buy vegetables from Tichaona to give him some pocket money as encouragement. I think digging and planting in the soil helped him work out some of his frustrations, and it certainly kept him busy. He said he liked being at Melfort because he had a place to sleep, he was able to go to school, and he had food. Later he said he wanted to be a mechanic. I hope that worked out for him. I don't know where he is now, but I feel sure his future is much brighter than it would have been without Christ in his life.

In order to stay at Melfort, the kids were not allowed to come into town, and they had to attend school regularly. I estimated that about two-thirds of them did stay at Melfort, but some kept coming back to town to beg and would get into trouble. It was interesting that several of the kids on the streets, kids who had decided not to move out to the farm, would report to Joan and me if they saw anyone from the farm back downtown. Then we would have a talk with the child and see if he wanted to go back to the farm. We explained that if he did go back, we would see that he got a second chance, but he would have to stay there and attend school. (I admit that we did give some third and fourth chances!)

By that time, the PC(USA) and The Outreach Foundation were helping fund our ministry with the children. Many Americans were interested in this outreach work. Prayer is so important—we all know that—and the Bible verse "Pray without ceasing" is one of my favorites. I had been sending out prayer letters about what we were doing and including names of twelve to fifteen kids to pray for. I would say just a sentence or two about each one and add a prayer request, perhaps to stay in school or stop sniffing glue. These prayer letters first went to the congregations and individuals that were giving missionary support to Bill and me, but we found out that the letters were being passed around to others. Gifts of money continued to come in for working with these children at risk. With the first grant we got from PC(USA), Bill and I felt it was very important that we help Joan with some salary support. Joan lived very frugally, but she had been working caring for these kids for fifteen years with no regular financial compensation. She was an accountant and didn't want to give up that job, but in order to work with the kids she couldn't be employed full time. Joan was helping the children more and more, both in town and on the farm. So, Bill, with his financial acumen, helped me decide on a small monthly stipend for her, although she ended up taking less than we had originally intended. It allowed Joan to work almost full-time with *her* kids, as she sometimes called them.

Eventually, we realized that because Melfort was a government-run farm, it would be hard to rectify some things that were happening there. For example, when visitors came, those in charge would move the kids out of the dorms and into one room with mats so the beds would be available for the visitors. There were also problems with the way the lady who had been put in charge ran the farm. Because she had a brother who was in President Mugabe's cabinet, politics often got in the way. This situation was not good for the kids. Joan felt more and more that God's call to her was not to help at Melfort but to keep working with other kids on the streets. She continued to give the street kids tea and bread every morning and encouraged them to go to the school. Bill and I were able to help Joan with her ministry to needy children and their families by giving school scholarships. Sometimes we supplied rent money for single mothers or grandmothers, so the children they cared for would have a safe place to sleep. We were thankful that going to school was an option for some of the children, rather than begging on the streets for food and money.

Nevertheless, I continued to help with children at the farm and would take food out once a week. That's when I sort of "got into the middle of things" (not that I haven't been there before!). The kids were telling me that the food I brought to Melfort Farm was going out the back door. We would take out two or three large sacks of corn meal plus oil, sugar, tea, bread, and other items. When I checked, it became apparent that some of that food was missing. The kids would be fed a good meal perhaps two days a week, and other days they would get only tea and bread. I talked with the headmaster at the school, and he agreed the kids were coming to school hungry. So, I had a chat with the lady in charge of the farm. It was not a pleasant conversation. She insisted that the food was going to the children, that I was not understanding things, and that I was taking the children's side rather than listening to her side of the story. I had to ask her to forgive me. Nevertheless, I realized maybe we needed to give smaller quantities of food rather than once-a-week deliveries. There was a grocery store halfway between Harare and Melfort Farm. Mr. George, the owner, said we could give him money, and the people from the farm could come and get the food there. We decided that was probably a good plan. The farm had a truck by that time that someone had given them. We paid for the smaller quantities and asked Mr. George to check that only mealie meal and things that were for the children like tea, milk and bread were taken out. One of the big issues was sugar—those in charge of Melfort wanted a whole lot of sugar, and we said the kids didn't need that much sugar. Eventually we worked out a plan to send Mr. George a check every month. But still the food (or lack of it) always seemed to be a problem.

During this time, I would go out once a week and have a Bible study with the children. Often Paul Neshangwe or another pastor went with me. Along with prayer and Bible study, we had a time of singing and dancing together. When we first met these kids in 1994, we found that once we started meeting in church, they loved to worship the Lord. They would dance and sing with joy! They knew hymns and choruses, and they would praise the Lord by raising their hands and dancing around the fellowship hall at City Presbyterian. Out at the farm, they were continuing to do this. The boys really enjoying being freer and having a place to worship and go to school, or at least most of them did. We were never able to reach about one-third of the kids, and they were the ones causing most of the problems. Theft was frequent. Some kids would steal items and quickly sell them. We hoped and prayed that sexual abuse was not also continuing, but we were concerned about that. Several Zimbabwean doctors were helpful in going out to Melfort with us. Sometimes we tried to look into accusations, but when kids have lived on the streets, it was extremely hard to determine what was actually happening. Some doctors felt they could not treat the children without permission from parents or grandparents, and of course in some instances there were no parents in the picture. I was disappointed, but I understood the difficulty. Joan and I both got discouraged, but in our times of prayer together, Bill would remind us that even though things at Melfort were not what we wanted them to be, the kids were better off than they had been on the streets.

Even while living on the streets, some of the kids wanted to go to church with us on Sunday mornings. Joan had taken them to the Anglican Cathedral downtown, but sadly the Anglican congregation didn't make them feel welcome. Some kids had torn up property and this had caused hard feelings. We decided since they were meeting at City Church, that could be their church. City Presbyterian has a beautiful sanctuary and a rather affluent congregation. They had been gracious about the program, but we knew there were some who didn't want these children and this ministry to take over the church and become their main emphasis. Consequently, we tried not to draw too much attention.

One of the boys I especially loved, Rogers, asked if he could go to church with me. There were Sunday morning services at 7:30 and 9:00 a.m., and of course we chose the latter service since it's hard for children on the streets to get up early. I was not sure Rogers would meet me that first Sunday. The service was starting, and he wasn't there, so I went in and sat in the back of the sanctuary. As we began singing the first hymn, Rogers slipped in and sat next to me. I reached over and gave him a hug. The kids wore all of their clothes in any weather so that they would not be stolen, so Rogers was bundled up with several layers that morning. As the service progressed, I knew he was paying attention and listening to the sermon, but when it came time for the offering I planned to pass the plate past Rogers to the person on the other side of him. But Rogers put his hand on the plate and said, "Wait a minute." He reached down through several layers of clothing into his shirt and pulled out a coin that he had wrapped up. He carefully unwrapped that coin and put it in the offering plate, probably the only money he had—like the widow's mite. Tears filled my eyes and I looked away. I had not expected that Rogers would give anything, but I was wrong. For me, that was a moment of realization that God was working in his life. I realized I needed to be more sensitive to the Lord's leading.

Rogers was very smart. He had been in our school at City Presbyterian and then had moved to Melfort Farm, but I didn't realize how much his life had changed. He did very well in math and reading. On one of my visits, several kids were asking me to bring sweets and things like that, but Rogers told me there was something he needed badly: a dictionary. I brought one for him. He really wanted to improve his life. He used to tell me the Presbyterians had helped him a lot and changed his outlook. He hadn't liked his life on the streets. It was a hard way to live and sometimes he did things he was ashamed of. In spite of the freedom that life provided, he said no one would choose to live on the streets if they had somewhere else to go. I enjoyed seeing how Rogers matured and grew in his faith.

Lovemore Home

We had been looking for a house in the Harare area for a ministry to vulnerable children. (They don't like to be called street kids, so we just called them God's children.) Joan found a house on Lovemore Avenue in the Cranborne area of Harare in November 1995, but it took quite a while before we were actually able to take in children off the streets. The house had been a doctor's residence; he lived upstairs and performed surgery downstairs. It came on the market because the family was leaving the country and wanted the money right away. The house was beautiful, with a good bit of property around it. We asked the price and were told it was $52,000 U.S. I remember wondering where we could get that amount of money, but Joan, Bill, and I all felt that the Lord had chosen that house to be used for God's children. We put up a bid, and then began praying for the money. I mentioned to Bill about the possibility of calling Alex Booth, The Outreach Foundation (TOF) Trustee who had given funds for our program in Zaire. Alex had always been so generous to help with evangelism programs, training pastors, building schools, and ministering to needy children. Bill encouraged me to call Alex. I'd already informed Bill Bryant, the TOF Executive Director, about the house, and he had told me he would pray with us to find a way to purchase it. I called Alex on the phone the next day. The conversation didn't last more than two or three minutes. I explained that we had found a house we wanted to use for a ministry for vulnerable children, but we needed the cash up front. He said, "OK, that's fine, Nancy," and that was the end of the conversation! He agreed to put up half of the money, and TOF would raise the other half, although Alex advanced the full amount so that we could go ahead and purchase the house immediately.

I lay awake for the next several nights thinking, "What can we do with this house?" Bill, Joan, Paul and I prayed along with others on our team about how the house ought to be used. We decided it would be mostly for at-risk boys, because there were more boys than girls on the streets. We were involved in some programs for girls, but it is much harder to work with girls. If a girl became pregnant, we would have to find a place for the baby. Working with needy young girls is extremely important, but it is a special kind of ministry. We decided to limit the age of the boys to fourteen and under. Some boys we took in turned out to be older, because there were no birth certificates and with malnutrition, they looked younger than they were. Some also gave us false information about their ages.

It took us two-and-a-half years to get approval from the Social Welfare Department and the Zimbabwean government to begin using the house. As it was on Lovemore Avenue, we decided to call it Lovemore Home, because that was exactly what we wanted to do: give more love to these boys. We invited a Presbyterian pastor and his family to live upstairs in the house for the time being, but we had to get approval from the Health Department and the Child Welfare Department before we could bring in any boys. Problems with bureaucracy are common everywhere, but they are worse in parts of Africa, and especially in Zimbabwe. Nobody would sign off to give us permission. For one thing, we had to have plans with the Health Department about how we would take care of the boys in an emergency. Bill laughed when he heard this because the boys were living and working or begging on the streets, so it would certainly be better for them to be in the house than out on the streets. We already had gotten together a staff, and we needed to document information about them. We could understand that the officials wanted to know about adults who would be living there and taking care of the boys, but the red tape seemed overwhelming.

Across the street from Lovemore Home was an Air Force barracks, called the Second Brigade, and that was one way God helped us with security. There was a government school nearby for the children of families living at the barracks. One day the head chaplain in the Air Force, a wonderful Christian man who knew of Joan's work, invited Joan and me to meet with him. He said, "I see in your heart that you want the best for these children. We want them to come to our school. We thought you were going to move children into the house right away. Can the children begin school next week?" We explained the government permissions we needed from many departments. The chaplain was instrumental in helping us cut through a lot of that red tape. What an answer to prayer he was! We were also excited that the school the boys would attend would be a community school, a good school. How gracious and generous of this man of God to say they wanted to be a part of what we were planning to do with Lovemore Home.

Finally, there were only two hurdles left. First, we had to run an ad in the local paper saying what we were planning to do in order to see if the neighbors had any objections. Second, as expats, Bill and I could not own the house, and anyway we didn't want it in our name. The Outreach Foundation didn't want it deeded to them. Bill suggested that we put the deed in the name of the UPCSA (Uniting Presbyterian Church of Southern Africa, Presbytery of Zimbabwe), a decision that would mean giving the house to them. The Presbytery put the proposal to a vote. In the end, the Presbytery voted to accept the deed and the house. Lovemore Home was opened on April 21, 1998, with five boys living there.

We had intended to fly back to the United States mid-May to receive an honorary doctorate from Montreat College but moved our flight up to be with my mother who was quite ill. Even though I did not get to see her, I was able to have a wonderful conversation with her before she died on May 10th. On May 15th, we flew to Montreat, North Carolina, for the Montreat College Commencement the next day. At the ceremony, Rev. Dr. Howard Eddington, chair of the Board of Trustees, said many kind words. We were surprised and honored by the award and by his comments as we did not feel we were doing anything special other than following God's leading. It was a bittersweet time for me with mother's passing to be with the Lord only 6 days earlier. We had her memorial service May 19th and returned to Harare later in the summer.

Maury Mendenhall had returned to Zimbabwe as a PC(USA) volunteer in early April to work for two years, spending a lot of her time at Lovemore Home. She helped us get the home ready and the boys settled in and enrolled in school. She also helped to train the Zimbabwean staff and worked with them almost on a daily basis. Maury is such a gifted, dedicated, and resourceful young lady. She grew very close to the boys at Lovemore. She took them places and arranged for other volunteers to come to Lovemore and work with the boys. Everyone loved Maury. The boys often told her things they wouldn't tell us. Bill and I felt Maury was like our second daughter. She was very knowledgeable about the problems that the kids on the street faced. She also taught in the school at City Presbyterian and worked with short-term PC(USA) volunteers who came to help. Our team certainly could not have accomplished all that we did without Maury. So, of course, we all hated to see her leave in the summer of 2000 when her two years were up.

It was just wonderful that in September 2000, Noel, one of the first children I had befriended, was among the boys we took into Lovemore Home. He had fallen behind in schoolwork, but not too far behind. He would piddle around and not get to school on time. He had formed bad habits that were hard to overcome. We kept in touch with the school to check his attendance and progress in his studies. We had a good staff at Lovemore, and somewhere along the way one of the staff members got through to him. I had talked with Noel, but I knew my influence was not going to be as convincing as a Zimbabwean pastor or schoolteacher. Finally, in tears, he realized that if he did not attend school regularly, he would not be able to continue in school. We told him, "Noel, we can't keep paying for you to stay in school, to live at Lovemore, and to get uniforms, food and book bags unless you do your part and go to school regularly. The agreement at Lovemore is that you will stay in school and really make an effort." He got the message and by high school he was trying harder. Sadly, however, he didn't have a good base, so we looked for someone to tutor him. God provided a young Peace Corps volunteer working in Harare to tutor Noel when she was in town on weekends. With her help, he was able to bring up his grades. He eventually went to Mhondoro Presbyterian School and graduated.

Noel was still at Mhondoro when Bill and I left Harare in November 2001. Paul Neshangwe took an interest in Noel and helped him quite a lot. Noel just loves Paul! When I heard later that Noel had gone to Johannesburg, South Africa, to look for work, I got in touch with Paul. Paul went to seminary there and told Noel to get in touch with a Presbyterian pastor and let Paul know when he did. Then, if I wanted to help Noel, I could do it through that pastor. Noel did indeed go to church and his pastor sent me a couple of e-mails saying he would be so glad to be in contact with us and to help Noel. Noel wanted to go to school to be a chauffeur. Bill and I were going to send money to help with the classes, but it was much too expensive. Paul suggested that we tell Noel to return to Zimbabwe. I did as he advised. Noel came back to Harare and found an apartment and a job. He calls me regularly and even emails me periodically. I continue to pray for him and know God has a special plan for Noel's future. He recently sent me a photo of himself in front of the big eighteen-wheeler he's been driving. So, he finally did become something of a chauffeur.

When boys first arrived at Lovemore Home, we would try to get as much information as we could about their families and where they had lived. Those working on the Lovemore staff were assigned the job of trying to connect with members of the extended family or the community where the boys had grown up. We wanted to know where they came from and something about their relatives, even if the parents were dead. Most of the time, it was grandparents that we located.

Muzandiwa was another boy taken into Lovemore Home. I don't

know how many years he had been on the streets, but both of his parents had died, probably of HIV-AIDS. He had a grandmother whom we met later while he was living at Lovemore. She was quite elderly but loved him very much. He told us, "My life was never very good. No one ever wanted me except my grandmother, and she was too poor to buy food and pay for schooling." Muzandiwa remembered that his mother wrapped him in rags and left him in a beer hall. That may be true; I don't know. Maybe she knew she was dying of AIDS and had no one to leave him with. Sadly, that happened frequently. Many children's memories of their mother or father weren't good ones. The name Muzandiwa means "unwanted child." He said he hoped someday to be called Amon, which means "someone good."

When Muzandiwa came into Lovemore Home, he fit right in and was never a problem. He always went to church and was very polite. He loved soccer and was an excellent player. When representatives from some of the national soccer teams came around to the schools to see kids that had some talent, Muzandiwa was one they looked at. They wanted him to work out and practice with the junior teams (similar to a high school team). He had to have a uniform and soccer shoes, so we got those things for him. He was excited about the uniform and the shoes, and he practiced faithfully.

At Lovemore, Muzandiwa would volunteer for whatever job needed doing—washing dishes or whatever. I remember praying with him and telling him, "Muzandiwa, it is just wonderful that you are willing and happy to do whatever anyone asks you to do." He would answer, "I'm so thankful I'm here." When he first came to Lovemore he didn't smile very much, but in the two years he lived there we saw him blossom as he experienced God's love. He was happy to be in school and to play soccer. Eventually the Black Rhinos U17, a professional football team for players under seventeen years of age, invited Muzandiwa to join, an honor that gave him tremendous self-confidence. But even more important, Muzandiwa learned to be a part of the family of God and through that experience to understand that he was special because Jesus loved him, and we loved him. I thanked God for Muzandiwa.

After living two years or so at Lovemore, Muzandiwa went back to the village to stay with his grandmother. He was happy with these arrangements. Lovemore staff and the Presbyterian Children's Committee agreed to pay for his schooling. He went on to finish high school. I pray he is married now and a happy young man with children. That is what he wanted.

Emanuel was another child we were able to get into Lovemore Home. A favorite of ours, he was eight or nine years old at the time. His father had served as a soldier during the war in Mozambique and died before Emmanuel was born. Emmanuel lived for a time in a squatters' area in Epworth, a particularly poor suburb on the outskirts of Harare, with his mother and maternal grandparents. Both grandparents were visually impaired and survived by begging in the City Center of Harare where his mother earned a meager living by selling vegetables. Emmanuel would sometimes accompany his grandmother to the streets to beg, serving as her guide. As he grew older, he began to wander away from his grandmother and she, unable to locate him, would return to Epworth at the end of the day without him. Thus, he started to spend more and more time on the streets, singing and dancing to get coins from people. His name was Emanuel, "God with us," and he did know God loved him. It was amazing that so many of these kids knew about God. They would say, "I know about Jesus Christ and He's right here with me on the streets." The problem was they didn't really understand that Jesus loved them or even that they were lovable. They didn't know that Jesus was there to help them change their bad behavior and self-destructive tendencies.

Emanuel said the dangers on the streets were terrible. "Some kids get beat up or get hit by cars. Some end up sniffing glue—and you know that can make you lose your mind. If the streets are the worst place in the world, then Lovemore is the best." He must have stayed at Lovemore one of the longest periods, maybe three years, because he was young when he came in. Even though he was eight or nine, he was put in first or second grade because he hadn't been to school much, but he shot right up to the top of the class. Emanuel was everyone's favorite because he could sing and dance. He had leadership abilities and a ready smile with a twinkle in his eye. His teachers told us they loved him, and he really put forth the effort to work and study his lessons. They appreciated the way he was striving for order in his life and working to become a different child. He wanted to have a bright future.

The Lovemore Home staff found Emmanuel's mother and encouraged him to reestablish a relationship with her. A couple of times he ran away from Lovemore, back to the streets to see his

At Lovemore Home with the boys and the staff

mother, and we would go and get him. I don't think his mother ever really took him back into the family; I believe she may have been troubled mentally. Thus, he was enrolled in a boarding school for a time, which Lovemore Home paid for. I hope he has been reunited with some of his family. At Lovemore Home, Emanuel developed incredible skills and self-reliance; his self-esteem went up quite a bit. He memorized many Scripture verses. He helped me learn some of the songs the children loved to sing. When asked to sing a chorus and dance, he was always exuberant, with a genuine, contagious smile. I believe Emanuel was the child who told me, "If you give me a slice of bread, that's kindness. If you put jam on it, that's *loving* kindness." He definitely was a Christian, and he could really pray! My prayer for Emanuel is that his life is better, and he is living for Jesus. One of my memories of Emanuel is of him singing and dancing jubilantly, with one shoe on and one shoe off. We had a video of this and every time I saw it, I laughed and laughed.

Home of Hope

Joan Trevelyan found some of the boys who came to live at Lovemore Home. She knew them all. Today Joan is still doing full-time ministry on the streets. Her program cares for several smaller children (paying school fees, rental fees for their mothers or grandmothers to have a roof over their heads, etc.). Thanks to The Outreach Foundation, she's currently living in a house in downtown Harare and using a second house on the property for ministry to women and children who are vulnerable, needy, hurting, and poor. She has a new car, not brand new, but new to her. Also, her son Craig left his job as a graphic designer to join his mother full-time in this ministry. Craig and Joan are two of the most amazing people Bill and I have ever known. Joan is certainly in the mold of Mother Teresa of Calcutta—one of the closest to Mother Teresa we've ever known. Maury Mendenhall and some of the young people who have worked with her called her St. Joan, but Joan did not like that at all. So, they just said it when she wasn't around.

Joan calls her ministry Home of Hope. She has been harassed by government officials and has been told to stop feeding and otherwise helping children and mothers from the streets. However, she knows God has given her this responsibility, and she does it joyfully. I think right now of the sweet smile on her face and the twinkle in her eyes. Joan taught me early on that we could not give the kids money because they would use it for glue, cigarettes, or beer, but she could always give them a hug. Joan and I gave out lots of hugs every day. On rare occasions we did give the kids money if they had to go to the clinic or hospital, but they had to bring back a receipt so we would know they had gone for treatment. And sometimes we would give the youngest children transportation money in order to get them off the streets, especially before dark, if we knew they had a place to go. Some of the children had an uncle or an auntie or somebody who would allow them to sleep there at night after they came into town to beg.

One of Joan's regrets is that it is so difficult to help men. When men are homeless, it's often because they feel they cannot go home for fear they will be looked upon as a failure. Many homeless men and women in Zimbabwe are taken to prison where they suffer harsh treatment. Because prison conditions are so bad and the political situation is not good now, Joan feels that she cannot go to the jails, although there was a time when she visited jails quite often.

Police have hauled off truckloads of men, women, and children from the city center and dropped them in remote areas miles from town. Those who make it back to the city show up days later with very sore feet. Most of the children made it back to the city after having walked hundreds of kilometers on foot, but some were attacked by wild animals or died trying to cross flooded rivers. Riot police call them trash. They have little mercy for these children, hitting and whipping them for no reason when they find them on the streets. One policeman stated, "These street kids are a nuisance! We should just kill them all!"

On one occasion a group of boys was taken to the police station when they were seen playing soccer with an obviously new and expensive soccer ball. "You couldn't possibly have a ball that nice unless you stole it!" they were told. In order release the boys, Joan had to carry a sales receipt to the police station to prove to the officers that she had given the boys the ball.

Joan hands out clothes and blankets when she can, particularly for the children. Bill and I sometimes helped with this, especially when the weather got cold in the dry season. However, people will steal shoes, pants and blankets while the children are sleeping. Sometimes the children pee in their clothes intentionally so that others won't steal them. Joan's ministry continues to provide scholarships for school fees although some mothers won't let their children go to school because they need them to beg in order to have some income. Another problem that prevents children from going to school is the requirement of a birth certificate, which is almost impossible for street children or orphans to obtain.

Because President Mugabe was embarrassed by the long lines of hungry people showing up in the capital city, Joan ran afoul of government officials on many occasions. One time she and Craig were taken forcefully from their home in a truck and driven to a nearby army base. Joan made her anger known in no uncertain terms. She led the group that had been arrested with her in singing hymns, and that made her captors very angry. She told them, "I'm praising the Lord in Shona. There is no law that says I can't praise my God. You know, God loves you, too!" Joan and Craig were kept under arrest overnight. When told she would no longer be allowed to feed needy people, she retorted, "My God is telling me I should feed the hungry. You are telling me not to do it. To whom do you think I should listen?" Understandably, the men at the police station could not think of a good answer for that one!

Miraculously, in spite of gas and food shortages, Joan and her team are still able to procure twenty loaves of bread each day. She uses her car to find items to help people in need. She gives out vegetables and bananas from her yard. "Someone might starve today while there is food here," she says. "If we don't give them something, they will steal. Then they'll be picked up for theft. It's not easy for people to come to Zimbabwe now, especially Americans. The government is extremely rude. But if it were not for American Christians, we would be dying in the thousands. We can sense some days that people are praying to keep us going."

Joan and her staff work with thirty-five to forty-five women. Some are totally illiterate, yet they learn to use patterns, make buttonholes, and sew simple garments. Joan gives them seed money to buy fabric and teaches them how to set the cost and how to anticipate inflation. There is always a spiritual message for those who come, and Bibles are handed out to celebrate the completion of a sewing course. One of the women Joan helped was a member of the Apostolic Church. Apostolics are not allowed to read the Bible. Joan told her, "People have died to bring you this book. How can you not read it?"

Home of Hope has a caring staff. Lucy, one of Joan's talented and enthusiastic helpers who loves the Lord, lives with her son in the second house on the Home of Hope property. Her husband died of AIDS several years ago. She is HIV positive but remains willing and able to work with Joan.

Dave and Ria Rock are also an important part of the Home of Hope team and a great help to this incredible ministry. Ria was the secretary/administrative assistant at Highland Presbyterian Church, the largest and most affluent church in the presbytery, a congregation that has been very generous in helping the poor over the years. Ria's close friendship with Joan developed on the tennis court, when one or the other would win the tennis championship in Harare. Dave, now retired, had been the general manager of a large fertilizer plant, overseeing a thousand employees. Joan asked Dave in April 2001 to help with accounting and paying bills. He thought the job would entail an hour or two each month and readily agreed to help. Bill knew the job would require a lot more than a few hours and began putting aside $250 in the budget each month in anticipation of supplementing Dave's retirement income. Since we left in November 2001, Dave has handled electrical problems, licensing, some of the purchasing, maintaining the automobile, writing reports, telling stories for donors, resourcing when items are hard to find, and maintaining the corporate bank account.

Dave and Ria also meet visitors and help serve the people in this ministry. Providing food during times of inflation has been difficult. "We've become hunters and gatherers," Dave said, "bartering, trading, and buying wherever we could. We've gotten through with the help of the Lord. Without the Lord and The Outreach Foundation, it would have been impossible." Dave and Ria have even driven to South Africa to buy supplies at a cheaper price. "We try always to be good stewards," said Dave. "We never want someone to come to Home of Hope and think we're being wasteful." He and Ria are a

**Home of Hope team: Dave Rock,
Joan & Craig Trevelyan and Ria Rock**

huge source of help and encouragement for Joan and Craig. What a wonderful team they are, serving the poor and marginalized in the name of the Lord! We pray weekly for Joan, Craig, Ria, and Dave. They flesh out what it means to serve Jesus faithfully and joyfully. We thank God for them and what they do for "the least of these."

Two Pastors of Faith

Paul and Lydia Neshangwe and Pattison and Susan Chirongo are two exceptional couples that God has used in a mighty way in Zimbabwe to grow His church. Paul and Pattison, both wonderful Presbyterian pastors, are like sons to Bill and me. Sometimes they call me "Mom" or "Gogo" (Grandmother in Shona) and Bill is "Mufundisi" (Pastor in Shona). We've known both men since 1994 when we moved to Harare. Paul serves in the Presbyterian Church of Zimbabwe, and Pattison in the Church of Central Africa Presbyterian (CCAP). God works through people like these two dedicated pastors, called by God to serve as disciples of Jesus Christ. At one time they both served churches in the city of Chinoyi. We thank God for them and for the tremendous church growth that has taken place and is continuing in sub-Saharan Africa.

Zimbabwe is one of those countries where the church is growing, even in the midst of hardship and suffering that was inflicted on the people by their former president, Robert Mugabe. People are hungry; they come to church because it is a center of hope. They understand that in the church they are received and loved by God. Romans 5:3–5 means so much to them: "We rejoice in our sufferings, because we know that suffering produces perseverance; perseverance character; and character, hope. And hope does not disappoint us, because God has poured out his love into our hearts by the Holy Spirit, whom he has given us." They know that God understands their pain and distress because Jesus Christ, God's only Son, was sent to die for them. He understood poverty and suffered in the way that they are suffering. Jesus endured this, even though He did nothing wrong.

Many African Christians understand that they are sinners and live in a fallen world. They have taught me that suffering, pain and oppression are not what they seek, but they know it refines, purifies and brings them closer to Jesus Christ. Many have written about "the company of the suffering." In Africa we have seen how, due to the severity of the HIV-AIDS pandemic, nearly everybody is touched by pain, suffering, and personal loss. In addition, greedy and corrupt leaders have brought terrible hardship to countless millions of Africans. President Mugabe declared war on his people, just as President Mobutu did in Zaire. The citizens of Zimbabwe have gone through a dark and difficult period since 2000. Whenever we ask Lydia or Paul, Susan or Pattison, or others on the front lines of dealing with these problems, "What we can we do to help?", they always answer, "Pray for us. Don't forget us in our hour of need." That's pretty humbling. They're not asking us to come over there and solve their problems, but to stand with them as brothers and sisters in Christ in their time of hardship and their hour of need.

Pattison's story is compelling. He had a congregation in Harare when we moved there in 1994. Over time we grew to know and love him and his wife, Susan, both committed and winsome Christians. Pattison's father was a foreman on one of the big farms in the Chinoyi area in May 2000 when President Mugabe allowed the "war veterans" (actually gangs of thugs) to settle on farms, take over the homes, and confiscate or destroy whatever they wanted.

In this case, it happened to be a white farmer who owned the farm where Pattison's father worked. The farmer and his wife were not living in the country so Pattison's father, who was crippled, actually ran the farm. Pattison told us that as the war veterans descended on the farm and said they were taking it over, his father told them, "The owner is not here; he's out of the country. I'm the one in charge. I cannot give you the authority to take over this farm." He begged them to wait and leave something in writing that could be sent to the owner of the farm.

The war vets carried guns as they confiscated farms and were often drunk. One day a group of them drove up and cursed at Pattison's father. First, they made fun of him and threw him around a bit; then they made him run nine miles into town, even though they could see he was crippled, while they followed behind in cars and trucks. When Pattison's father got into town, he was exhausted. He had a stroke, and his heart was affected. Pattison said what a terrible injustice this was. His father was such a wonderful Christian, respected in the community and chosen by the white farmer to live there and oversee his whole farm.

Through Pattison's eyes, Bill and I have seen and heard a lot about the suffering that has been wrought on Zimbabweans by President Mugabe in the years he was in office, especially since 2000. Unfortunately, Robert Mugabe remained president until 2017 when he was finally made to step down at the age of 93. He left the country and its people in desperate circumstances, but they graciously allowed him to remain in their beautiful land and live out his days in luxury until his death in 2019.

Pattison has had problems with his government for many years. He was asked to be an election observer in 1995. A thin and wiry man, his blood pressure shot sky-high as he watched officials bring in a boxes of pre-marked ballots one night during the election. He said, "I can no longer be an election observer or do anything that involves my government. I get so angry that my blood pressure is affected."

Pattison is handsome, articulate, and one of the most honest pastors we've ever met. He has a wonderful sense of humor. Bill and I are thankful that he received the opportunity for further seminary training at Justo Mwale Theological College in Lusaka, Zambia. His wife and family stayed back in Chinoyi during this period. Susan is not ordained, but she more or less ran the growing congregation while he was away. She ended up preaching, teaching in the school, leading the women's group, and even doing funerals. There were a great many funerals during that time because of the HIV-AIDS pandemic, and also because starvation was a problem. Susan said representatives from the government would come to her church every Sunday to listen to the sermons and make copies of the church bulletins to see if they could catch her or anyone in the congregation making statements that would allow them to make an arrest. Susan and Pattison have both been followed by the CIO (equivalent to our CIA). These years of suffering have taken a toll, but their strong faith in Jesus Christ and the fellowship and prayers of people who care about them have sustained them. Pattison later served as Moderator of the CCAP in Zimbabwe.

Paul Neshangwe also has a gripping story. He tells his own story in a powerful way:

My name is Paul, and I am here to tell you the story about my life and how God transformed my life to be the way I am today. Currently, I am a pastor with the Uniting Presbyterian Church of Southern Africa. I was not born to Christians. I was born to parents going to church every now and then.

The year I was born my father took a second wife and had a son with the second wife. Two sons were born in the same year—myself and my half-brother. The other son was born before me. My half-brother was given a name that his mother did not like. When I was born, I was given my father's Christian name. From that time on there was a serious problem in my family, because my step-mother did not like the fact that I had been given this name. The name Paul was special because it is my father's baptismal name. To have a father or grandfather's name in our culture is quite an honor. As anyone would guess, when these two wives meet, married to one man, there are bound to be problems in that family. In my case my father went on to marry two other women. He had four wives and more than twenty children. There were problems among the wives. My father's family was in turmoil most of the time, fighting for survival—basically, survival of the fittest.

My father was in the Rhodesian army. Zimbabwe became independent in 1980. My father was an employee of the Rhodesian army as a soldier so it was compulsory for us to go to church. We were forced as little children to go to church, but we did not like it.

Also, because of the problems in our family, we did not like our father. I hated my father when I was growing up and felt that he was a cruel, uncaring man. He did not treat my mother in a respectful manner. I hated all the things he stood for. I did not like the white people he was working with. He adored them. I hated white people. I hated the women he liked. I hated Christianity. It was his idea that we would "catch" the Christianity of the white man. We began to believe as little boys that we should work against Christians. Around 1980 the Zimbabwean government became independent after a war and began pursuing communism and its principles. We were excited about communism, so Christianity had no place in our lives.

There were many problems in our family. At ten I started drinking whatever I could get my hands on and smoking, just to get the frustration out. For me, 1986 was the year everything got worse. Also, it was a turning point. I got a new life. In 1986 I couldn't face life anymore. I tried to kill myself three times because life was too painful. The family was fighting and my father stopped giving support. Life became meaningless. I thought it best to get drunk and kill myself. Thank God I did not succeed. Three attempts to kill myself did not succeed. I concentrated on being naughty and on criminal activity.

But also in 1986 in the little town where I lived I saw posters going up advertising the Jesus Film, about Jesus' life according to the Gospel of Luke. My friends and I were enraged and thought we should keep them from telling about Jesus, even through posters. We didn't want anything to do with the white man and his religion. So we pulled down the posters hoping to ensure that people would not watch this film about Jesus.

On the day the film was showing, I went to watch this film. I was not interested in seeing it. My desire was to disrupt what was going on. My friends and I tried to disrupt the proceeding by making noises and being rowdy. The members of the Presbyterian Church who were showing this film did not try to stop us but left us to ourselves. When nobody comes to stop you, you quiet down on your own.

The film was progressing. During the time that time Jesus was cleansing the Temple, a voice said to me, "Suppose what you are watching is true, Paul?" From that time on everything changed. The figures I was seeing on the screen were like real life characters. Something was happening to me—something I could not explain. I remember by the time Jesus was nailed to the cross, I was in tears. When my friends saw the tears, they thought I was upset that these people were showing the film.

At the end of the film all who wanted to be Christians were invited to come forward. I stood up and went forward. My friends stood up with me and also went forward. The people at the front of the church explained how one could become a Christian. They prayed with us and asked for our addresses. I gave my right address; my friends, false addresses. As we were leaving, my friends were making fun. How dare these people think we would give proper addresses? I couldn't admit to my friends that I had given the right address.

The following Monday when I woke up, I was conscious of the presence of God. There was something about this Christianity I couldn't run away from. I couldn't figure out what it was. I couldn't work it out, but God was real in my life. I couldn't tell my friends at that time. So, as I was with my friends, this excitement and whatever I had in me began to cool. Toward the end *of the week some people from the Presbyterian Church came to our house to follow up on me. When I saw the pastor's car parked outside, I said, "Oh, no." I asked my sister and her friend to tell them I was not there. I hid. They didn't try to stay. They left pamphlets and encouraged the people who were there to read them and to give them to me. Then they left.*

October 1986. From that time on, week after week the people from the church came looking for me. Family members kept coming up with stories that I was not there. I would go to the back of the house. The church people never gave up but kept looking for me. In December we moved to a new house because my father had sold the house where we had been living. I went to stay with my oldest brother, far away. But again, the people from the Presbyterian Church never gave up. They kept looking for me. In March, somehow, they found me. I was ready by that time to accept that God was real. There was something about this Jesus. I could not run away. I was ready to become a Christian. My brother and I were hungry, something that was normal for us. We had gone three or four days with practically nothing to eat—only drinking water. On the day the church people came we sat around the table in my brother's house. I was ready to say, "Just tell me how to become a Christian." I can't explain. Something happened to me. I had seen this film of Jesus being crucified. I was ready to say He is real. The pastor used an illustration in talking with us. He put his hand in his pocket and took out a Zimbabwe dollar (and in those days it could buy a lot). He said to my brother and me, "God in heaven is a free gift. We do not deserve to be given this salvation, to be saved by God. It is something he does out of his love and it is free." Then he said, "Paul, it is like this dollar in my hand. I want you to have it. Take it. It is yours. I am giving it to you out of love. That's the same way God gives us salvation." My brother and I looked at each other. It was so strange that a stranger would come and give us money. Now we could buy bread. We prayed with these Christians and gave our lives to Christ that day. We went out and bought bread, came back, and ate bread with so much joy.

We said to each other, "This is heaven to us—a free gift." From that day on my life was transformed in a number of ways. The pastor who was leading the group looking for me was a white man. When he explained Jesus, when he spoke to us, it did not matter that he was white. It was as if God had opened my eyes to a new reality. I began to see him as a person and to listen to him. Something changed in my attitude about race. One thing I know: with God, skin color doesn't matter.

I still hated my father. When I accepted Jesus, my father did not change. He was still the same old character. I didn't work through that problem for a while. Then when I was training to be a pastor, preaching on forgiveness, God confronted me about my hatred for my father. I was going to mention in the sermon that God asks us to forgive those who wrong us, and that God should forgive us the same way we forgive those who trespass against us. God wanted me to challenge the people in the church: was there was someone in their lives not yet forgiven. As I was preparing, I realized that I had a problem. It struck me that I had not forgiven my father. I made a decision that day to forgive him. I needed to communicate to my father that I had forgiven him. Also, I must communicate the way I saw Jesus being crucified on the cross as I watched that film, the way I understood it all by reading the Bible, the way Jesus was crucified for my sins and for my father's and anyone else's. If I kept on holding a grudge against my father and was bitter toward my father, I would be saying that Jesus' death was not enough, that I wanted some special punishment beyond Jesus' crucifixion. And so I communicated to my father that I used to hate him but did not anymore. Now I love him because of what Jesus has done. Now I am at peace. My father has not changed that much, but we are together and pray together. His life style has not changed much; his attitude toward my mother leaves a lot to be desired. But I just trust that the price Jesus paid for my father is enough for his wrong. I pray that he will get to the place that I am, that he will know the love of Jesus. Jesus forgave all the things I did, the drinking, bullying, and pulling down those posters.

As I have already said, I did not like women. To me, women were less than men, less than human beings. God confronted me on this attitude and challenged me. I began to see women as people, even Father's second wife. They are precious people for whom Christ died. As I grew in my knowledge of God and in my love for God, I realized that the price Jesus paid is so great that both women and men have to be special. The Bible says we are co-heirs. Because I am grateful to God, I began to relate to ladies as my sisters. I am grateful that at age twenty-four I met the lady who is now my wife. I have a healthy perspective of ladies. I am married and love my wife dearly. Again, this is all because of that day watching that film when Jesus challenged me.

I thank God that he used the experiences that I had thought were negative before becoming a Christian. God used all those things to preserve my life. He protected me from going with many girls. This saved me, when one considers the HIV-AIDS problem that is now destroying Africa.

In sub-Sahara Africa, the HIV-AIDS problem is very serious—a crisis. Many members of my family have been affected—brothers, sisters, a number of relatives. As a pastor I have buried family members and many other people. Young children are being left with no mother or father, no one to take care of them. I could have been like my brothers or any one of us who is either sick or now dead. I am the fifth brother in the family. Four of my brothers are dead, most from AIDS. I believe I could have been one of them. God has a way of working out everything to produce something good.

I tell my life story because the most critical thing for me is to go out into the world to share with others how God has touched my life. He touched it in a way that I wish many people who went through what I did could get to the point where they know that Jesus was crucified in order that they may have life. No one can ever take away my life in Him. It is painful to bury loved ones. I have comforted my father's family, in-laws, and members of my congregation. I know what it is to lose loved ones. I do not *focus on death. I now know that in Christ there are better things to come. I know that when death comes, death is not the final story. I know people can have life and have it abundantly.*

I pray that others—blacks, whites, men, women—will know what I know. When Jesus died, he had each one of us in mind. In Gethsemane, before Pilate, while being crucified on the cross, people told Jesus, "Save yourself." But Jesus replied, "Father, forgive them, for they know not what they are doing." What he had in mind was forgiveness for them, for Paul, for every person, that every person may have life. In spite of the hurts, God loves me. God forgives my sins in Jesus.

Before he came to the Presbyterian Church in Chinhoyi, Paul was chaplain at Mhondoro Secondary School, an outstanding Presbyterian school located about an hour outside Harare. He became one of the main leaders in helping street children after working with our program at City Presbyterian and then serving as the Chairman of the Board of Lovemore Home. He and Lydia are a gifted and dedicated couple who had a wonderful ministry to the students at Mhondoro.

With Paul Neshangwe

At the height of the land chaos in 2001, when the white-owned farms were being taken over by the supposed war veterans, Paul received a call to be the pastor of the Chinhoyi Presbyterian Church. The original congregation was mostly white, many of them farmers now being deprived of their land. Now the neighborhood around the church had changed and was 96 percent black. Paul debated and prayed long and hard before accepting the call to this congregation. He was concerned for his personal safety, but even more worried for Lydia and his children. Yet he felt God asking him, "How seriously are you concerned about these people?"

Months before, Paul had met a white farmer, Jim Steele, a Presbyterian elder and lay pastor whose daughter-in-law was dying of malaria in a Harare hospital. The presbytery called for a minister to pray with a dying woman, and Paul happened to answer the call. Jim and Paul became close friends. Jim was one of the main reasons Paul made the decision to accept the call to Chinhoyi. Jim and his wife, whom Bill and I also came to know and admire, were members of that congregation.

By way of background, Jim Steele's father came to Zimbabwe from Scotland in 1926 and bought the land he farmed. Jim was born in Zimbabwe. Paul once told Jim, "You should hate the people who took your land. If you can do the unexpected and love them, what a witness that will be!" So, Jim plowed the land for the men who had taken over his farm and taught them how to work the land that he was no longer allowed to farm.

Interestingly, the Chinoyi Presbyterian Church has stayed at about a 150 members, but the membership has changed dramatically. As the white farmers were thrown off their land, many of them moved to Harare or went elsewhere. The white families who remained now worship beside the black members who have taken over their farms. Both of the country's political parties are represented in the congregation. They have two services on Sunday mornings: in English at 9:00 and in Shona at 11:30. Once a month, they combine the two for communion. Working to overcome racism (racialism, as they call it) and dealing with broken families and neglected children have shaped Paul's ministry. He stresses love and preaches about the need for reconciliation with God and with others. It hasn't been easy for him to minister to whites who were losing their homes. Because he's black, some white members at first thought of him as one of "them," the enemy. It has been a great joy to see white and black members having communion together, taking tea afterwards, and discussing together the problems caused by hunger and famine. Naturally, some whites said the congregation had changed too much and decided to leave. But a small group has seen the miracle of God's power. There are now more blacks than whites in the English worship service.

The government does not want whites and blacks to mix. In fact, at the time Paul came to Chinoyi, every half hour there were tirades on the radio trying to keep the groups at odds. The government would say, "We tried reconciliation at Independence, and it didn't work." (Zimbabwe, the former Rhodesia, became an independent nation from U.K. in 1980 after much fighting and violence.) Paul is always thankful when God brings the races together. In June 2001, the church ordained new elders: two white and five black, the first black elders in that congregation. This racial change wasn't done just to please or placate anyone, but because it was the right time, and they were the right people to lead this integrated congregation. The police asked Paul why the English service was first. They felt it showed preference to whites. Paul said, "Come and worship with us. You'll see we don't give priority to anyone."

Under Paul's leadership, the Presbyterian Church partnered with other churches to serve the hungry in the Chinoyi area. The church building was not used much during the week since people being displaced from their land now had to drive greater distances to get there. People came twice a month for food, mostly people who were caring for children who had been orphaned due to the HIV-AIDS pandemic. There were many families being helped by that program.

Infiltrators came to the church occasionally to check up on Paul. His phones were tapped for a time and CIO questioned him, "only because we are friends" they told him. He knew the real reason: the government did not like to see people being fed by non-government providers.

In August 2004, only three days after Paul's second child was born, the church offices were destroyed by fire. It was started by petrol bombs and was politically motivated. The office and Sunday school rooms were damaged. Fortunately, the fire did not get into the beams leading to the church sanctuary. Norman, who had worked at the church for twenty-two years, had put money in the church safe, the entire year's income from his wife's work in the family's fields. She had just sold her crops for the year, and all that money burned in the fire.

Paul's response to the fire was to say, "Well, Jesus said that in this world you will have trouble. I suppose we should expect these things as long as we are on this side of heaven. We are troubled but not destroyed." It turned out the government party, Zanu-PF, had offered an evangelist in the church certain things in order to help with the fire. Of course, he wound up getting nothing. In a forgiving spirit, Paul invited him to come back to the church in spite of what he had done.

Because Paul continued to speak out against the injustice and suffering caused by President Mugabe and his cronies, he was on a list of those Mugabe wanted silenced. So, Paul took his family and left the country for five years. He went to Colorado, where he was invited to serve on staff in Denver Presbytery while Lydia attended Denver Seminary. They are now back in their beloved country of Zimbabwe.

Zambia, Mozambique and Madagascar

During the years 1994 to 2001, Bill and I also worked in Zambia, which borders Zimbabwe on the north. We made the eight- or nine-hour drive from Harare to Lusaka, Zambia's capital, too many times to count.

On our first visit in October 1994, we met Elder Munjongo and Esther Namuyamba in Siavonga, Zambia, a remarkable couple who were caring for orphans. Munjongo had an important job, the number two man at the large Kariba Dam power plant located on the border between Zimbabwe and Zambia, on the Zambezi River. Esther worked as a nurse/midwife in the nearby hospital. They are dedicated Christians, highly respected by all who know them. They often invited Bill and me to stay with them, and our friendship blossomed over the years into a very special relationship. We quickly came to appreciate Munjongo's wonderful sense of humor and Esther's delicious cooking, and we enjoyed getting to know their extended family. It was always a blessing to be with them. Bill felt very honored when their first grandchild, a son, was named William.

We worshiped several times with Munjongo and Esther at the Siavonga Presbyterian Church, where we met many dedicated members and witnessed tremendous growth in this congregation. We were impressed that a large number of young people were joining. As the membership increased, the congregation was able to build a much larger church that now sits on a hill overlooking the town of Siavonga. Funds for this project were given through The Outreach Foundation from caring Presbyterians like our friends Henri and Candace Rush along with many others in the U.S. We took several Presbyterian groups to visit and worship with this congregation. There is a beautiful plaque on the wall of the church expressing the members' appreciation for the help they received.

Munjongo has an interesting personal story. His father died when he was four. As often happens to widows across Africa, his father's family came in and took away everything in the house, leaving his mother with nothing. She soon remarried, but his stepfather made Munjongo drop out of school and tend his cattle instead. The next year Munjongo found a Christian teacher who agreed to take him in as a houseboy in return for an education. At the age of twelve, Munjongo left his village in order to attend secondary school. To reach the new school, he walked alone for three days, carrying his suitcase on his head. When night came, he would ask the chief of a village for permission to sleep there and continue his journey the next morning. At the new school, he did janitorial work and learned to mend shoes to earn some money that he used to buy a camera. He began to photograph other students. The money he earned paid for the education of his younger half-brother and half-sister, as well as his own tuition. At last, Munjongo graduated from college and married Esther. For many years he was the head accountant for the huge hydroelectric dam that provided electricity for Zambia and Zimbabwe. He and Esther took in orphans throughout their marriage, even though they had six children of their own.

Namumu Orphanage Center

Munjongo took early retirement from the power company in 2001. He and Esther left behind their comfortable government housing to start Namumu Orphanage Center (NOC) with assistance from The Outreach Foundation (TOF). We were so thankful that TOF Executive Director Bill Bryant was interested in helping Namumu succeed. It became home for nearly eighty orphans and vulnerable children. Chores such as gardening and tending pigs taught the children practical skills and brought in some revenue. Those students who were weak in academics got tutoring and were trained in carpentry, needlework, or other skills. The goal was to help them learn a skill so they could be independent when they left Namumu. A chicken project was started to help with the nutritional needs of the children. Later, more income was generated when a couple of fishing boats were purchased for kapenta fishing on Lake Kariba. Kapenta is a small, finger-size fish, plentiful in the lake and a popular source of protein (although recently kapenta have become less plentiful).

The chapel was the first building to be built at NOC in 2001 and is the center of the campus. There the Namuyambas taught the children about the love of Jesus Christ. A welcome addition was the building of a community primary school on the property for grades one through seven. A small medical clinic was built later and overseen by Esther for several years. The one-room clinic is very basic, but it continues to serve both the children at NOC and people in the surrounding community. Several babies have been born there.

Munjongo and Esther worked hard to get the school accredited by the Zambian government. As a result, the government provided a principal and two teachers. Other teachers came from the community. The school soon had over 300 students. Bill and I were very encouraged to see many of the students from NOC grow spiritually as well as academically. While the Namuyambas were present, weekly chapel services were held with a strong focus on biblical learning and following Jesus. The children loved to sing Christian songs and act out Bible stories. Every time we visited, they would entertain us by singing, reciting Bible verses, and dancing. I can still see their smiling faces and remember how much we enjoyed being with them! The children loved it when we brought balloons, colored pencils and paper, bubbles to blow, and games to play. Of course, we also brought footballs. Football, as soccer is called there, is the national sport all over Africa!

Muhange, a beautiful young girl we first met when she was living with Munjongo and Esther, was a distant relative of theirs. She was sent at age eight to live with them because her mother had died, and her stepmother didn't want her around. They loved her like their own and she blossomed. Muhange was gifted and extremely bright, and she loved the Lord. A natural leader, she spent over four years at Namumu and became the "head girl." She was always spending time with the younger children and teaching them songs,

Bible verses, and games. In a special play put on for us by the children, she recited these heart-rending words:

Look at me. And don't be scared. For I am an orphan.

Brothers, look at me and think twice.

Find a solution to look after me.

I move on the streets looking for food. Dustbins are my playground.

Rainwater is my shower. A sack is my mattress.

Please help me.

Is it a sin to be an orphan?

Malachi Habasimbi came to the Namumu Orphanage Center (NOC) in 2004 as a young boy from a poor family. Some doubted that he would succeed, but Mujongo and Esther nurtured him and told him that Jesus loved him. I remember that he enjoyed singing and loved the stories about Jesus. In the summer of 2013, Bill and I, along with Peen Hardy, made a visit to NOC. Malachi told us that he wanted to be a pastor and work for God. We did not realize just how gifted Malachi was until we attended the worship service Sunday, July 28, at St. Marks Presbyterian Church. Bill had been asked to preach. Peen and I were in the congregation, along with several of the young people from NOC. Malachi played the keyboard and directed a youth choir as they sang "There's No One Like Jesus". Peen and I were invited to join in as we all danced and sang together. When it came time for Bill to preach (in English), Malachi was asked to translate into Tonga. It made our hearts glad to see how God was using him. We were so thankful that he received a scholarship through funds given to The Outreach Foundation and went on to study for 3 years at Justo Mwale Theological College. He is now an ordained pastor in the Presbyterian Church of Zambia. It is amazing how God has worked in the life of Malachi.

Christopher Kasanda wanted to be a medical doctor but came from a very poor family who couldn't even afford to feed him. His dream seemed impossible. This changed when he was sent to the Namumu in 2004. We met Christopher shortly after he arrived.

Over the next ten years, we watched him mature as a Christian, excel in school, and become a leader at the orphanage. Because he finished in the top ten percent of all students in Zambia on the secondary school exams, he was accepted into college for medical training. Scholarship assistance from Presbyterian individuals and congregations in the U.S. allowed him to pursue his life-long dream. I was so pleased that my home congregation, Park Lake Presbyterian Church, gave generously to help Christopher and other graduates from NOC continue their studies after high school. Among these was Florence Chisangano who also pursued medical training. In 2020, Florence & Christopher returned to serve as clinical officers (similar to nurse practitioners) at the Namumu clinic. Who would have imagined what God would do in their lives! There are many other children like Muhange, Malachi, Christopher, and Florence. The Namumu Orphanage Center has offered them the opportunity to grow up in a safe Christian environment where they could recognize their potential and realize their dreams.

**Graduates of Namumu making a difference
(Christopher, Victoria, Florence and Malachi)**

Zambia is a peaceful nation with rich natural resources. Some statistics say that nearly seventy-five percent of the population is

Christian. Half the population is sixteen years or younger. Yet it is also a country where nearly seventy percent of the people live in abject poverty, often existing on one or two dollars a day.

In the area around Namumu Orphanage, there were over five thousand orphans and vulnerable children who had been abandoned or whose parents had died of AIDS. During one visit, we met and talked with a group of churchwomen who had very little for their own families. Yet I was touched that these women took time to bake scones to sell in the marketplace to raise money for families who were struggling financially because they had taken in orphans. Sadly, many women are left behind to care for their families alone, because their husbands have gone to Lusaka or another city to find work. The men aren't able to return home very often. Many have sex with prostitutes, become infected with HIV, and when they can't continue to work, they return to their village, often infecting their wives before they die. The AIDS pandemic has changed life for the African family. A child may help nurse his or her father until the father dies and then have to nurse the mother, knowing that she will die too. Children who survive this ordeal have many challenges—the burdens of poverty, grief, fear of the future or, more frequently, hopelessness about the future. Munjongo expressed his dismay when someone asked, "How do you preach about a loving God to such a child?" He replied, "The only answer is for those of us who are Christians to show them God's love through our actions and compassion. God wants to love these children through us." Over the years Munjongo and Esther have served as parents and grandparents, not just for their own family members, but caring for and sharing the love of Jesus with many, many other "little ones." We thank God for both of them.

HIV-AIDS and the Crisis Nurseries

In our time living in Africa, we became more and more aware of the problems facing the multitude of children whose parents were dying or had already died from AIDS. The statistics are staggering. At one point it was reported that 13.2 million children in sub-Saharan Africa have been orphaned because of this disease, including 900,000 orphans in Zimbabwe alone.[vi] Some of them were single-parent orphans, having lost a mother or a father, and some were double orphans, having lost both parents. Girls in particular have had to bear heavy responsibilities caring for sick parents and younger children, depriving them of the opportunity to go to school.[vii] In 2002, the United Nations estimated that one in three adults in Zimbabwe were living with HIV. The rate hasn't really declined; more people with HIV are living longer and there are still new infections, so many people are still living with HIV.

In our December 2002 newsletter we wrote, "The reality of what faces our African sisters and brothers in Christ at this time is heartbreaking. At the International AIDS Conference in Barcelona, Spain, in July 2002, AIDS was declared a global security threat by the U.N. Security Council."

In response to the emergency, the World Health Organization and the United Nations (UNAIDS) launched a global initiative to provide HIV medicines to three million people living with HIV in developing countries by the end of 2005. The Zambian government was very willing to ask for assistance and collaboration from the international community as they confronted this public health crisis known as the AIDS pandemic. In 2003, the U.S. government launched the President's Emergency Plan for AIDS Relief (PEPFAR), the largest commitment of international funding to any specific disease.[viii] The plan focused initially on 15 priority countries around the world; Zambia was one of the 15 initial countries while Zimbabwe first received funding in 2006. The commitment of international funding for HIV, combined with increases in the Zimbabwean government's domestic budget dedicated to health and HIV, successfully reduced new HIV infections, reduced AIDS-related deaths, and strengthened systems and structures to help address the social and economic impacts of AIDS on children and families.[ix] In Zimbabwe, the life expectancy at birth had plummeted from sixty-one years in 1985 to only forty-three years in 2004. As a result of access to HIV medicine, the life expectancy finally reached 1980s levels again by 2015.[x]

We have met many grandmothers who have had to raise their grandchildren. African Christians have been stepping up and caring for the many orphaned and vulnerable children. We are humbled that God helped us be a part of starting a ministry in Zambia that is caring for children impacted by AIDS. I think of Mother Teresa describing herself as "a little pencil in God's hand—merely His instrument—writing His love letter to the world." The story of how the crisis nurseries began is an example of how God does incredible things when people are willing to be "a little pencil in God's hand."

While attending a conference in England in 1998, I met Dr. Phyllis Kilbourn, a remarkable missionary with Worldwide Evangelization for Christ International, who worked with needy children and authored several books about children in crisis. She connected us with Jennie Woods and Sandra Levinson, friends of hers who founded an organization called Alliance for Children Everywhere. Bill and I began a wonderful friendship with these two amazing ladies. They told us they were working with the Christian Alliance for Children in Zambia (CACZ). They were praying about the need for a crisis nursery in Lusaka, to rescue small children and babies who were abandoned or whose families were unable to care for them due to the death of one or both parents. Bill and I talked with Bill Bryant to see if there might be donations to help with starting such a project. Bryant is a visionary, a compassionate and dedicated man of God. He was very interested in this project. Thus, began a partnership between The Outreach Foundation and CACZ to care for orphans in Zambia, which at that time was labeled the "world's epicenter of AIDS orphans." During this period, I often cried when I heard the stories of many of these orphans and their unbelievable suffering. Psalm 40:8 came to mind. "I delight to do your will, O my God," I wrote in my diary as I worked to find a solution to some of the suffering.

It was wonderful to see how the Lord was moving people, especially Christians, to meet the needs of these vulnerable little ones. Bill and I are thankful for all on the original team who came together for prayer and planning to start a crisis nursery in the poorest part of Lusaka. Sandra, Jennie, and their Zambian team soon found a suitable house in the Kanyama neighborhood. It was purchased with gifts from The Outreach Foundation and Presbyterian congregations in the United States. The team worked tirelessly to transform the house to get it ready for receiving and caring for babies and small children. The new Kanyama Crisis Nursery was dedicated on September 22, 1999. Bill and I drove up from Harare to be present.

I was thrilled that little Stanley Chiwama was one of the first children taken in. I had met him during an earlier visit to Lusaka. He was about two years old, very small for his age, extremely malnourished. It was painful to see this listless child sitting in a small chair with such tiny little arms and legs. But I will never forget the first time I met him because, as I entered the room, he raised one hand to wave to me. With that gesture, he captured my heart. I brought some biscuits (cookies) and bananas for him and for the other children present. Stanley took the food and wolfed it down. Thereafter, I always brought biscuits and other food with me when visiting the Kanyama Crisis Nursery to share with the children, but especially with Stanley. When his parents first brought him for help, they didn't acknowledge that he was theirs. They said that he belonged to someone else. We later found out they both had a drinking problem. It was obvious that they hadn't taken care of Stanley. Because his family was not able to adequately take care of him, Stanley remained at the nursery for about three years. I was known as his "granny" and saw him when I could. All of us who loved him were so pleased that he was able to attend a nearby elementary school run by the Salvation Army where he did well in his studies. Later he was placed in a Christian group home where Bill and I continued to visit him. It was so comforting to see him grow and respond to the love of his Christian caregivers. I still pray for Stanley and thank God for all those who have taken care of him.

Two more Crisis Nurseries were started in Lusaka by CACZ with the help of Sandra Levinson and Jennie Woods. In August 2000, the House of Moses was opened to care for babies and very young children who were in need of a "safe haven" until they could be placed in foster care or adopted or, in some cases, returned to family members who were now able to care for them. On November 16, 2003, the Bill and Bette Bryant Crisis Nursery was dedicated in honor of Bill Bryant's retirement from The Outreach Foundation (TOF). It cared for vulnerable children from ages two to five. We were pleased to be present for the dedication of these nurseries, along with Bill Bryant and several visiting Presbyterians from the United States. Eventually, one more home was opened for older children, the House of Martha. The majority of generous funding for all these homes was provided by Presbyterians through TOF. These crisis nurseries have saved the lives of many vulnerable children.

Bridget was one of the most courageous children I've ever met. Orphaned at eight, she was a sad little girl who became the head of her household, caring for her four-year-old brother, Joseph, and her eight-month-old baby sister, Catherine. Both of her parents had died, probably of AIDS, but she had no time to grieve their loss. She took her siblings to stay with an auntie; however, there wasn't enough food in the house for all of them. So, Bridget began a daily journey on the bus to the crowded, garbage-strewn paths of the Soweto Market in the heart of Lusaka where she begged for food. She would lovingly tie Catherine on her back, take Joe by the hand, and off she would go. Many people reached out to help her along the way. The bus driver let the children ride free. Thankfully, one day a Zambian Christian secretary who worked for UNICEF found them wandering in the market. She took them back to their home and soon realized that the "aunties" were indifferent to the children. She offered to take Bridget, Joe, and Catherine to the Kanyama Crisis Nursery where they could receive loving care. There was quick agreement about this. At first, Bridget didn't want to let anyone else take care of Joseph and Catherine but seeing that her siblings were being well cared for, Bridget finally agreed to stay at the nursery and go to school. She was placed in the third grade and quickly became one of the top students in her class. Bill and I met Bridget when she first came to the Crisis Nursery. Whenever we came to Lusaka, we visited with her and were pleased to see her blossoming and happy. We enjoyed watching her play games with the other children and hearing her sing about Jesus' love.

James was another precious Zambian child whose life was turned upside down while he was still young. He went to live with his auntie shortly after the death of his father. His mother had died the year before, but he could still remember her face and her smile. He was an only child, which is very unusual in Zambia. The little family of three had been very close. James loved school and had been the brightest child in his second grade. Everything was different now that James was an orphan, living in a strange house. There were lots of people in his auntie's house, but no books or games. He missed being in school and felt very alone. One morning James was pleased to be invited to go shopping with his auntie. He didn't recognize the street or the neighborhood where they went, but nonetheless he was happy to go on an outing with her. That day his life changed. His auntie told him to wait by a rock. James waited patiently. And waited. He was tired and hungry and had to go to the bathroom, but still he waited for his auntie to come back. As the hours passed, James began to wonder if his auntie was ever coming back. He tried not to cry, but it was starting to get dark. He was cold, alone and scared. Finally, courageously, he asked a kind-looking passerby if she knew where there was a police station. In school, he had learned policemen are your friends. Late that night James was driven in a police car to the Kanyama Crisis Nursery where he found a comfortable warm bed in a room with six other boys. In the morning Mama Nellie, a staff person, came in, sat on his bed and listened to his story. When she reached out to hug him, he finally cried.

James surprised Nellie and the other nursery workers when he volunteered to pray during devotions on his first day. "Dear Jesus," he said, "thank you for this good house where I can live. Bless Auntie and her house, and help all of us to love you, Lord." Shortly thereafter, we were visiting in Lusaka with a group from the PC(USA) and TOF. We were touched when James asked if he could pray for us. He thanked God for our visit and said we had blessed all of them at the Crisis Nursery by coming. We thanked him and prayed for him. He spoke to us about one of his favorite Bible stories, about

Moses who was chosen by God to help the Israelites and lead them out of Egypt. Thereafter, we called him "the little preacher."

James needed a mom and dad. He stayed at the Crisis Nursery for a short period until a family from the U.S. asked to adopt him. We were so pleased to learn this news. James had grown very close to Lucy, a little girl at the Crisis Nursery. He said she was like his sister and he didn't want to leave her behind. The family decided to adopt Lucy also. What a wonderful answer to prayer!

Justo Mwale Theological College

At the same time, we were working with the Namumu Orphanage and the Lusaka crisis nurseries, Bill and I were also involved with Justo Mwale Theological College (JMTC) in Lusaka. This outstanding institution equips pastors and church leaders for the vibrant, growing church in Zambia and beyond. The college was named in honor of Justo Mwale, who in 1929 was the first Zambian to be ordained by the Reformed Church in Zambia.

Over the many years we worked in southern Africa, Alex Booth, Bill Bryant, and The Outreach Foundation (TOF) funded several projects that greatly improved the JMTC campus. My Bill was the point person for working with the college on these undertakings. Alex graciously funded most of the projects, which included improvements to the administration buildings, the addition of a new library in January 1998, an upgrade to the water system, and construction of a hostel in 2001 for visitors and those taking short-term courses. The Centre for Continuing Theological Education, which officially opened in March 2000, was financed by the Booth Family Africa Fund and was named for Alex Booth. It was a privilege for Bill to partner and work with several principals of JMTC: Rev. F.D. Sakala, Dr. Rian Venter, Rev. D.T. Banda, and Rev. Edwin Zulu.

We first visited JMTC in October 1994. Bill met with Rev. Sakala who told us the college was operating in the red and could not get accreditation until it was financially viable. Bill worked with Bill Bryant and Alex Booth to help the college pay down the debt by building income-generating houses to rent on the campus. Funds were also raised for the Alex Booth Lay Training Centre and TOF guesthouse. Much of what has been achieved at Justo Mwale over the past twenty-five years can be ascribed to the continuity of service and the outstanding number of well-qualified and dedicated teaching staff.

On September 14, 2001, Justo Mwale celebrated fifty years as a theological college. They honored both Bill Warlick and Alex Booth by awarding them recognition of Outstanding Service. The administrative staff noted that Bill's dedication, encouragement, and perseverance helped Justo Mwale Theological College reach its full potential as an accredited joint ecumenical theological college. We were present for this celebration with our daughter, Elizabeth Turk, and her family. Alex Booth was not able to be there, but several years later he finally got to visit Justo Mwale with Bill and me. The staff and faculty thanked him and honored him with a large birthday cake and joyous celebration on his 77th birthday. The school is now known as Justo Mwale Theological University College and there are students from seven African countries studying there. Through TOF and PC(USA), Bill helped organize scholarships for theological students from Zimbabwe, Mozambique and Malawi. He believes that Justo Mwale Theological University is one of the foremost theological colleges in Southern Africa.

While serving as Southern African Coordinators for The Outreach Foundation from 2002–2014, we were pleased to be invited twice to return to Justo Mwale, to live on campus and work with the faculty and students. During the first period, Bill served as part of the interview team that hired Rev. Moses Mwale to coordinate the Booth Lay Training Centre. They also hired a full-time caterer and a bookkeeper. What a joy it was for us to see how the program at the Booth Lay Centre was expanding. Dr. D.T. Banda was the principal of JMTC during this period, a dynamic and dedicated leader and teacher. We got to spend time with D.T. and his wife, Monica, also a pastor. It was inspiring and encouraging for us to interact, worship, and pray with faculty and students as well as their spouses. We witnessed again and again how God was moving in the hearts and lives of the seminary students and their professors.

Our congregation in Orlando, Park Lake Presbyterian Church, was supporting Kingstar Chipata, who was from Zimbabwe, as he studied at JMTC. Bill and I were impressed with his dedication to the Lord. Kingstar was away from his family, who were back in Zimbabwe. Sadly, one morning while we were on campus, Bill heard that Kingstar's wife had died suddenly of malaria. He found the young man grieving the loss of his wife and preparing to return immediately to Zimbabwe to be with his family and to plan for her funeral. Bill was able to pray with Kingstar and give him some money to purchase a bus ticket to get back home. Kingstar finished his studies and returned to Zimbabwe. He is a gifted and caring man of God. He eventually remarried. In 2010, he was elected General Secretary of the Church of Central Africa (CCAP) Harare Synod.

Mozambique

Thousands of refugees returned home after nearly fourteen years of war for independence from Portugal. That was followed by sixteen years of a deadly civil war. Thirty years of unending fighting and violence made this country the poorest in the world from 1992 to 1998. A recently returned Mozambican refugee described his plight during a BBC broadcast in May 1995: "We still sleep like rabbits … with one eye and one ear open." When we visited Mozambique, we saw the terrible destruction caused by the war—to churches, schools, houses, roads and infrastructure. Land mines had been planted extensively. Many men, women, and children were maimed or killed when walking across fields full of these mines. We also witnessed the suffering of so many and saw firsthand the poverty of the people. We heard vivid stories about the damage done to the human psyche by war. We hurt for those we met and with whom we worshiped.

Inkson was a young Mozambican who lived in Zobue, near the Malawi border. During the war he was injured when a shell from a bazooka exploded nearby. Only sixteen years old, Inkson was severely traumatized. He lost part of his hearing and was terribly scarred, both mentally and emotionally. He didn't speak, smile, or communicate for a very long time. Eventually, however, he accepted an invitation to worship with the members of Ampande Presbyterian Church and was baptized there. Some of the women in the church told us that they had feared they would lose Inkson because of his severe injuries. They understood what he needed. The evangelist told us that the congregation had literally loved this young man back to life. When we worshiped at Ampande, we were advised not to shake hands when we greeted him. He did smile at us, although it was a rather painful, furtive smile. The church members have helped him understand what Jesus was saying in John 15:4: "Abide in me, and I in you. As the branch cannot bear fruit by itself, unless it abides in the vine, neither can you unless you abide in me." Jesus wants to rebuild shattered lives. He came that we might find a home in him.

We have never had to live in a land where, if you missed the sounds of approaching rebels at night, it could cost you your life. For years, the Mozambican people lived like this, and we met many who had to flee from their homes not once or twice, but numerous times during the war. Most of those in Tete Province fled into nearby Malawi, where they found refuge. It was in the crowded refugee camps that many heard about Jesus Christ and his love for them. The Church of Central Africa (CCAP) in Malawi sent pastors, evangelists, and lay leaders into these camps to pray with the refugees and lead Bible studies and worship services. Consequently, many of these displaced Mozambicans accepted Jesus Christ as their Lord and Savior. When the fighting stopped, the door opened for thousands of refugees and families to return home between 1992–1994. The United Nations brokered a peace in Mozambique in 1992 and enabled a peaceful election to take place in October 1994.

One man who returned home at this time was Elder Yeretsami Kamangeni. He and the members of Ximpacho Presbyterian Church expressed great joy the day the ribbon was officially cut by Rev. Siamo Chimango, the General Secretary of the Presbyterian Church of Mozambique. The doors of their new church sanctuary were opened on December 9, 1996. Rev. Chimango dedicated two other completed church chapels at Tchessa and Ampande, both in the Zobue area, on that trip. The Mozambican Presbyterians in the area expressed appreciation for the help of PC(USA) and The Outreach Foundation (TOF) in building these three new sanctuaries. We were privileged to be present for these celebrations.

Elder Kamangemi was instrumental in the rapid church growth that took place in the Zobue area of Tete Province in Northern Mozambique. He has been a strong and dedicated Presbyterian lay leader in the Ximpacho community. When he returned home to Mozambique in 1994, he worshiped at the Tchessa church, but soon he felt the need for a Presbyterian congregation in his own community. He worked diligently to begin a new church in Ximpacho. Then, serving as a lay evangelist, he helped and encouraged the people to build a permanent church structure.

The elder and his wife have endured a great deal of suffering and loss of family members due to the many years of war in their homeland. Twice they had been forced to flee with their family and live in a refugee camp in nearby Malawi, from 1971 to 1974 and again from 1991 to 1994. It was there in 1972 that Elder Kamangemi accepted Christ as Savior through the witness of a Malawian Presbyterian pastor who had come to preach in the camp. He was given a Bible and attended a Bible study. Then, with another elder, he started a Presbyterian congregation for Mozambicans in the camp, which grew so rapidly that it soon divided into two church groups.

Elder Kamangemi and his wife lost ten of their thirteen children between 1971 and 1995, yet they have been faithful and joyful Christians. Their personal story reveals the tragedy caused by political upheaval and war. No one should have to go through what they have endured, but their resolute faith in Jesus Christ has brought triumph in the midst of pain and severe loss. The elder was known in his community as one who stood firm in his Christian belief, always rejoicing in hope, a modern-day Job who could say with assurance, "For I know that my Redeemer lives" (Job 19:25).

It is always a blessing to cross cultural and language barriers to share Christian fellowship and acknowledge the love of Jesus Christ that binds us together. We have experienced this often in our many years in Africa. We've also been privileged to introduce visitors from the U.S. and see them have this same experience.

Bill was encouraged to see the work expanding in Mozambique and new congregations starting up. Although many of the refugees returned to find their houses destroyed, they were pleased to be home and, at last, to have peace in their country. We were thankful that donations were coming from TOF and the PC(USA) to help with building more permanent places for worship. Each local congregation was required to help. They molded and burned bricks and collected sand and gravel or rocks for their church building. There were donations given for the construction of a school at Tchessa and several bore-hole wells to provide clean water. Bill soon realized their need for a full-time, dedicated pastor with a missionary heart, one who knew the language in Tete.

Rural church in Tete Province

In April 1995, Bill visited the Theological Education Extension center (TEE) in the Copperbelt region in northern Zambia. He met with Rev. Charlie Thomas, the director, and asked him for a recommendation, a pastor who could train lay people to become Bible teachers and church leaders in isolated areas of Mozambique where the church was growing rapidly. Charlie recommended Rev. Nedson

Zulu, one of their gifted young trainers of trainers who spoke five languages and was finishing his time at TEE. Bill was introduced to Nedson and knew he had found the person he was looking for. Bill explained to him that we were working with Christians who had little or no training to become deacons, elders, and women and youth leaders in Tete Province. The PECGA program was helping to raise funds for such training, as well as constructing of places of worship. In 1996, Nedson Zulu made the 17-hour bus trip from Kitwe, Zambia, to Harare, Zimbabwe, to lead the first trainings using the TEE program.

Nedson then agreed to move his wife, Sarah, and their family to Harare, where he became pastor of the Highfield CCAP congregation. It was decided that he would travel to Tete Province once a month and hold trainings to develop lay leadership for the expanding Presbyterian congregations in that area. Some of the congregations were meeting under trees or wherever they could find a place to gather. Others were building simple, rustic structures, stick walls with thatched roofs. Not surprisingly, when the rains came, these structures didn't hold up well.

When Nedson started seminars in Tete, those who attended were so enthusiastic, they would bring their own food and sleep on the floor of the church where the training seminars were held. Through Nedson's leadership and Sarah's help, the work expanded and more churches began to spring up. There were so many needs—clean water, permanent church buildings, schools, clinics, Bibles, and hymn books—that the work became more holistic. Bill worked with Nedson to introduce the *Jesus Film*. A team was formed for showing the film in several villages in Tete. The response was tremendous. This film has become the primary tool used by pastors, evangelists and elders to bring people to a saving knowledge of Jesus Christ, not only in Tete Province but elsewhere in Africa and worldwide.

As the outreach in Tete Province expanded and grew into a holistic evangelism project, a community health component was added when Sebber Banda, Sarah's half-sister, joined the ministry in 2003. A registered public health nurse and midwife, she recruited and trained traditional birth attendants who act as midwives in the villages. She also trained village assistants who provide basic medical care for villagers who are not able to visit health clinics or a hospital. Additionally, she has recruited and trained a talented group of performers who act out skits that help educate villagers on disease prevention and critical family and social issues. These drama teams draw big crowds.

As of this writing in 2020, the training events continue and there are now eighty Presbyterian congregations, several schools, and a couple of medical clinics in Tete Province. A new training center with a kitchen, a dining hall, showers and toilets has been built at Tchessa, with twelve rooms for men and twelve rooms for women. Now it is possible to accommodate more people at one time for training in a better environment for learning.

Berry and Elizabeth Long, along with Tom McDow, take groups each year to Tete to see the work and the needs there. Berry and Tom are Trustees of The Outreach Foundation. In June 2018, Bill, then retired and living in the U.S., was excited when the Longs invited him to visit Tete with the Outreach group. On this trip, Bill visited places he had never seen before and churches that had been newly constructed. At one place where a school had been built, the drama team performed a skit on the importance of girls attending school. This wonderful trip was a time of mutual encouragement.

Sadly, Nedson Zulu passed away in November 2018 from complications of pneumonia. Shortly before his death, he had visited us in Florida. We had time together to pray and catch up on news of the work in Tete. He was a godly man who had become like a son to us. Now Sebber is coordinating the Holistic Ministry in Tete Province. Rev. Carlos Faquione, a pastor who had been working with Nedson and Sebber for several years, is ministering with her. We are thankful for the faithful work of God's servants in Tete, a ministry that has brought glory to God's name.

Madagascar

As the Project of Evangelism and Church Growth in Africa (PEC-

GA) also included Madagascar, we made many trips there while we lived in Harare. Years earlier, while we were still living in Zaire, Bill had made a trip to this large island nation and met Rev. Jean D'Elinivo, the dynamic director of the Department of Evangelism for FJKM (The Church of Jesus Christ in Madagascar). Bill helped Jean get a scholarship from PECGA to attend the School of Evangelism in Kinshasa from 1990–91. Despite the turmoil in Zaire in 1991 which led to our evacuation, Jean was able to finish his studies and return safely to Madagascar. Jean started his ministry as an evangelist, but sadly his young wife died, leaving him to raise their five children alone. He continued his evangelism work, however, and eventually was chosen to be director of the Evangelism Department. As we got to know Jean better, we appreciated his gifts and his burning desire to spread the Good News of Jesus Christ. He loved to joke with us. We formed a wonderful friendship over the years and were happy when he married a fellow pastor, Angele. Jean stayed with us in 2000 when he came to the States to speak to churches. We would often stay with Jean and Angele when we visited Madagascar. Jean called Bill "Papa."

My first visit to Madagascar with Bill was in 1994. Parts of Madagascar were like an island paradise with amazing plants and creatures found nowhere else in the world like lemurs and tenrecs. Other parts were deforested with many people living without enough food or access to safe drinking water. It broke my heart to see families living in these conditions. In 1994, Madagascar was one of the poorest countries in the world. Yet in the midst of these situations, FJKM was present. Recognizing the need of the people and Christ's call to feed the hungry, clothe the naked, and give water to the thirsty, FJKM had many ministries including 500 schools and a Development Department with rural dispensaries, an environmental program, and a safe drinking water program. We came to appreciate the depth of FJKM's vision and commitment to spreading the Gospel and engaging in ministries to meet people's earthly needs.

Traveling in Madagascar was a challenge. There were very few paved roads and those roads were full of potholes. It was also nerve-wracking as you never knew when you might encounter bicyclists, oxcarts, or people walking on the road. There were not many places for visitors to stay. A team member who visited on a trip in 1998 with The Outreach Foundation (TOF) described the experience as "grueling." Because of my asthma and bronchitis, it was difficult for me to take long trips with Bill and Jean. I was grateful that our daughter, Elizabeth, and her husband, Dan Turk, were in Madagascar.

From 1992–1995, Dan did his PhD forestry work at Ranomafana, and Elizabeth served as a volunteer with FJKM's health ministry. In 1997, they began serving as PC(USA) mission co-workers with FJKM's Development Department in the fields of environment and health. It was always a joy to see them and our grandchildren Robert and Frances when we came to Madagascar to work with the FJKM. We took several wonderful vacations together and saw creatures like chameleons and lemurs in rainforests. I once saw a tenrec scurrying to its home on the forest floor. When he was younger, Robert spent more time speaking Malagasy than English. He called Bill "Dadabe," Malagasy for grandfather, and me "Bebe," Malagasy for grandmother. The church leaders loved hearing this, and Bill became known to them as "Dadabe" after that! Our grandchildren still call him "Dadabe."

When Bill was off on trips with Jean, I would stay with Elizabeth and her family and visit other FJKM projects. While staying in the capital city Antananarivo, I was struck by the number of small children living and begging on the streets. They were more numerous and much younger than the children on the streets in Harare. A ministry that really touched my heart was FJKM's outreach to the poor, needy, and marginalized. The champion of this ministry was Pastor Helivao Poget. She is an amazing woman of faith with great compassion and boundless energy. Elizabeth first introduced us to her in 2002 as she had gotten to know Helivao while they were working together on the FJKM's AIDS committee. At that time, Helivao was director of Akany Fifampandrosoana Ambodin'Isotry, a joint FJKM and Lutheran ministry for homeless children and families. The Isotry center is in one of the poorest and most populated parts of Antananarivo. It offers housing to some orphans and children who cannot be cared for by their families. About 60 poor children come for school every day. Older children are taught skills such as sewing in addition to regular classes. Church services are held each Sunday for street children and their families. Twice a week, about 300 children come for a meal and Bible study. We visited the center many times, and it was touching to see the children stream in off the streets, some of them carrying their siblings on their backs. Watching the little ones line up so well-behaved with their bowls of different colors and sizes for their beans and rice brought tears to my eyes. Even though they were hungry, they did not push and shove. On one occasion, Bill and I saw a little girl share her bowl with her baby sister. After everyone was fed, then Helivao or a co-worker would share a Bible story with them and teach them songs. After about three hours, the children would head back out onto the streets. It was heart-breaking to see them go, but it was good to know that they had a safe place to come twice a week where they were fed and could learn that Jesus loved them.

Helivao's heart for the marginalized led her to start a unique ministry to prostitutes. She calls them "ladies of the night." Part of this ministry involves walking the streets at night to talk with them and share about God's love. Helivao collaborates with a downtown church that opens its doors one evening a week so the ladies of the night can come and have someone to talk to and pray with. She trains seminary students in this special outreach, and they walk the streets with her ministering to these ladies. Helivao is fearless and says that God protects her when she is on the streets. She says that it takes several talks with the ladies before they believe that someone really cares and that changing their life is possible. For those who are ready to leave life on the streets, Helivao offers a place to stay, training, and help in finding a new job.

I remember vividly my first night walking the streets with her. The streets were dirty and poorly lit. Helivao had seminary students with our group so that we were not alone. We saw a lot of ladies waiting for clients. One came up to me and grabbed my arm and said, "Donne-moi de travail." I speak French and understood she was saying, "Give me work." I invited her back to the church for prayer and she came. I was moved that she wanted to sit with me. I began praying with her in French and then found a seminary student who could pray with her in Malagasy. I often wonder if she was one of the those who decided to leave life on the streets. It was a remarkable night that I will never forget. Helivao has since expanded her ministry with the FJKM to include fighting against human trafficking. Of all the people we have worked with, Helivao in Madagascar and Joan in Zimbabwe remind me the most of Mother Teresa with their tireless care for those the world has forgotten and abandoned.

The commitment of the FJKM to evangelism and church growth was inspiring and a joy to support. At one point, FJKM was starting a new church every week. The *Jesus Film* in Malagasy is a wonderful evangelistic tool which the FJKM Evangelism Department started using under Jean's leadership and still uses to this day. PECGA supplied the Evangelism Department with copies of this film.

Jean and Bill traveled the length and breadth of this unusual island by car and boat, visiting and encouraging pastors and evangelists, meeting with congregations and looking at sites where FJKM wanted to start new church developments. On one memorable trip, they had to cross a river in a dugout canoe, walk knee deep through a pond, and ride for an hour in a twenty-five-year-old land cruiser. When they finally arrived at the church, the congregation was holding a training for lay leaders. The men and women attending the training slept in the church or in nearby homes and brought and cooked their own food. The training lasted for three days and was part of a three-year program held twice a month on weekends. Books used in training, one book per year, cost one dollar each. When Bill asked how many people had books, only one person raised his hand. PECGA began to raise funds to supply these books. Each of the 36 FJKM synods conducts these training programs. Having trained lay leadership is extremely important, because FJKM has fewer than 2,000 pastors to serve more than six million members in over 6,000 churches (2019 statistics).

It was exciting to see pastors and lay leaders not only serving the congregations to which they were assigned but also going out and starting new churches in nearby villages. They have a heart for sharing the love of Jesus Christ with people. Bill hoped to *be* a blessing, but he came back from these trips having been blessed by the faith and commitment of those Christians he met.

In addition to building churches and training lay leaders and evangelists, we also worked with FJKM on some of its other priorities. This included raising funds for bikes and motorcycles for evangelists who served anywhere from eight to twenty churches in remote areas. Because most of these areas had no public transportation, evangelists would walk hours to reach their congregations. The bikes and motorcycles meant so such much to their ministry. PECGA also supported FJKM's four seminaries through building renovations, a library, training materials, and assistance to seminary students. One of the highlights when we brought visiting teams was worshiping at the Ivato seminary and meeting the students. Even though we did not understand everything, the students' joy in the Lord was contagious.

The lack of income for lay leaders and pastors was a big problem. Most of them did not make more than $50 a month, if that. PECGA helped finance a variety of income-generating projects based on FJKM's priorities. In the Mangoro Moramanga Synod, lay leaders and pastors were trained to raise chickens and pigs. The synod president, Pastor Jaona Rakotonindrainy, really impressed us with his organization and commitment to sharing the gospel. Jaona made sure he visited every one of the 145 churches in his synod. It took him two years to visit them all. Sometimes he traveled hours on foot. He crossed rivers to start new churches and had three centers for training lay leaders. In his ten years leading the synod, they started 100 new churches. In 2016, he was promoted to head the FJKM department that oversees all the synods, churches, and seminaries. In the Maevatsara Synod, a rice storage facility was built. When Bill visited this site again in 2017 after attending our granddaughter Frances' high school graduation, the storage facility was still working. The synod president said it was making a big difference for lay leaders, pastors and their families because there were many months a year that their congregations could not pay them.

In Miandrivazo, Bill got to know a bright evangelist, Rev. Tiana Alisoa Ranaivoniarivo, who was serving 21 churches. Over the years, Bill visited 19 of those churches. The PECGA project worked alongside local Christians to complete buildings for all 21. Recognizing people's poverty, Tiana said, "We can't separate spreading the Gospel and doing development work." Tiana's wife Anna was a great cook. Under Tiana and Anna's leadership, the church started a training center with PECGA funds that taught sewing, cooking, and pastry-making. Many people have earned income with the skills they learned at the center. It was eventually named the Bill Warlick School of Patisserie. Tiana later became head of FJKM Sunday Schools.

In 2007, Rev. Triomphe Randrianisaina replaced Jean as head of the Evangelism Department. In 2008, we visited Madagascar with another group from TOF and traveled with Triomphe. His gentleness and fervent dedication to spreading the gospel were evident to all. I remember his infectious smile as we traveled together to see evangelists in their villages. He took time to offer them advice about shepherding their flock and encouraged them in their challenging situations — many didn't have enough food to eat and had no electricity or indoor plumbing. Triomphe is also a visionary and is encouraging Malagasy Christians to use their own resources, no matter how small, for church planting and the work of the Evangelism Department.

The experience of one person who visited Madagascar with us sums up the contrasts you see in Madagascar:

> *One of my favorite stories from my trip illustrates the Malagasy's beautiful spirits. We had just arrived in a rural village by plane. Hundreds of Malagasy surrounded the plane. The children, dressed in beautifully vibrant colors and bare feet, hovered around the plane and stared at the strange Americans who had just arrived. I watched a young girl, no more than six years old, holding a six-inch peppermint stick. Without hesitation or*

prompting, the little girl took her treasured candy and broke it into three small pieces and shared them with two other girls. It was such an act of selflessness, but so completely indicative of the Malagasy people.

Throughout the course of our trip from village to village, we witnessed the hospitality and generosity of our FJKM brothers and sisters. Every meal that we ate was prepared lovingly and out of the limited resources available to the people. I'm sure the chicken and fish served to our small group could have fed each village for weeks.

We Americans arrived rich in material things, but we left richer in spirit by having learned from the Malagasy Christians about joy, hope, peace, and generosity.

Our FJKM sisters and brothers have taught us much about what it means to serve Christ. They embody what we see in many African churches – spiritual and physical ministries are intertwined. One cannot share the Gospel with someone and ignore his/her needs.

With Pastor Jean D'Elinivo overlooking Antananarivo, Madagascar

Returning Home

Bill and I left Harare at the end of November 2001 to return to the United States. Packing up and leaving Zimbabwe, and leaving Africa, was very hard for us, but Bill was almost 67, and we thought we should be looking at retirement. We have made many journeys in our lifetime, but this was one of the most difficult. We knew that it was time to go home, but Bill and I were deeply concerned about the deteriorating situation in Zimbabwe. Life was becoming very difficult for our sisters and brothers in Christ there. We were thankful for the many friends we had made. We had seen God's Spirit at work in a wonderful way and were grateful that we were able to partner with amazing Presbyterians and others in using the resources available from The Outreach Foundation and the Presbyterian Church for God's work. *How precious is your steadfast love, O God! All people may take refuge in the shadow of your wings.* (Psalm 36:7)

We flew back to Decatur, Georgia, to stay briefly at Mission Haven, where we had stayed during our furloughs. By Thanksgiving, after our routine medical check-ups as required for all PC(USA) missionaries, we had moved into my family home in Orlando, Florida. Bill's urologist, Dr. Max White, called to let us know that Bill had prostate cancer. It was a shock, but we prayed together and began looking at options. We did not know what the prognosis would be, so Elizabeth and her family came from Madagascar and William and his family came from Egypt to be together with us for Christmas. Bill decided to have surgery at Vanderbilt Hospital in Nashville in February 2002. Thankfully, Dr. J. Smith, a renowned surgeon with Presbyterian ties, was able to remove the cancer, and Bill did not have to have chemotherapy. We marveled at God's timing. Coming home when we did allowed the doctors to catch Bill's cancer early. Our retirement became official at the PC(USA) General Assembly meeting in Birmingham, Alabama, in June 2002. It was the end of an era for us and the beginning of a new chapter in our lives.

Bill and I were delighted when The Outreach Foundation asked us to continue to serve as mission consultants in Southern Africa, but to be based out of Orlando. We served in this capacity from June 2002 to December 2014, usually visiting Africa two or three times a year. In 2002, the Reverend Dr. Rob Weingartner became executive director of The Outreach Foundation. Bill and I were very pleased to be able to work with Rob and TOF for these 12 years. Rob went on a TOF trip with us in 2004 to Zimbabwe and Mozambique to see first-hand the Kingdom work being done with our African sisters and brothers in Christ. We had many adventures on that trip as we worshiped, prayed, and danced with Mozambican Presbyterians. Each group that we have taken to Tete Province in western Mozambique had many unique experiences, one of which was staying at the unforgettable Zobue Motel. The town of Zobue is on the border crossing with Malawi. While at this motel, Rob and the men traveling with us stayed in a very primitive back building with no electricity. He handled this with no complaints! Over the years, we have appreciated Rob's gentle spirit, servant leadership, and his role as a prayer warrior.

Serving as mission consultants with The Outreach Foundation was a very special assignment as it allowed us to continue to keep in touch and work with many African sisters and brothers in Christ. A PC(USA) and TOF brochure printed in 1986 contained these words:

We need your help. African churches are not looking for handouts. Indeed, our African partners contribute according to their ability and beyond. There still remain many obstacles and limits in Africa. Today, what our African partners urgently need are necessary resources, obtainable only with your help. Your contribution, no matter how modest, can help with seminary training, purchasing a bag of cement for a church building, helping obtain Christian literature for a Bible class, or helping provide a roof for a Christian school. The challenge is before us ...

Build a Church

Erect a School

Train a Church Leader

Spread the Gospel

Hand in hand we CAN directly help others half a world away.

Your contribution WILL make a difference.

Indeed, today we can say with assurance that Presbyterians have made and continue to make a difference with our partners in many countries in Africa. We have walked with our African sisters and brothers and served the Lord our God together. We have mutually encouraged one another through prayer and a ministry of presence. Together, we have learned the truth of God's word, *You show me the path of life; in your presence there is fullness of joy, in your right hand are pleasures for evermore.* (Psalm 16:11)

Bill and I have received so much more from our African friends than we have given. We have been inspired. We have learned from them how to *run with endurance the race set before us ... looking to Jesus the author and perfecter of our faith.* (Hebrews 12:1–2).

Wrapped in a gift blanket from the Presbyterian Church of Mozambique at our farewell ceremony—the traditional way of saying goodbye.

Epilogue

My mother Frances Kump Wooddell's love for missions and Africa has carried on for generations beyond hers. She finally realized her vision of being a missionary and spent two years as a teacher to missionary children in Congo/Zaire from 1967–68 and 1971–72. One of her daughters (me) became a full-time missionary serving in Africa for over 40 years. Her youngest daughter (Jane) also served a year as a teacher to missionary children in Congo/Zaire from 1966–67. Three of her grandchildren, Elizabeth, William, and Shamba, grew up in Zaire and one was even born there (Shamba)! All three worked in Africa with Elizabeth eventually becoming a missionary to Madagascar. Four of her great-grandchildren grew up in Africa and two were born there! Elizabeth's children, Robert and Frances, grew up in Madagascar and hope to work in Africa. William's children, Chloe and Jack, were born in Cairo, Egypt, during the six years he and his wife were teaching there. They hope to visit Africa after their studies.

Frances Wooddell
August 6, 1911- May 10, 1998

Heroes and Poems of Encouragement

In my lifelong adventure of faith, I have been encouraged by my family and my African sisters and brothers in Christ. There have been others who have stood out as heroes that have kept me going and inspired me when times were difficult. Here are just a few:

Mother Teresa: Her life of faith and care for those the world did not consider important have meant a great deal to me. Bill and I traveled to Kolkata, India. Though we didn't get to meet Mother Teresa, we were able to visit several of the houses run by the Missionaries of Charity where her presence was very evident. One poem that has encouraged me to continue on, even when there seems to be no change is *Do It Anyway.*[xi] The final lines remind me that I do what I do because God has called me to do it.

"Give the world the best you have, and it may never be enough;

Give the world the best you've got anyway.

You see, in the final analysis, it is between you and God;

It was never between you and them anyway."

Archbishop Desmond Tutu: His fight for justice, peace, and reconciliation in South African following apartheid meant a great deal. He has highlighted the need for forgiveness in his talks and writings. to me. His wife Lydia spent 3 nights in our home in Orlando at the invitation of my mother. It was wonderful to meet him in Kinshasa, Zaire, and be able to talk with him in person. I love his quote on neutrality and injustice. *"If you are neutral in situations of injustice, you have chosen the side of the oppressor. If an **elephant** has its foot on the tail of a **mouse** and you say that you are neutral, the **mouse** will not appreciate your neutrality."*

Bono, the lead singer of U2: His untiring fight to get justice for those with HIV and AIDS and to fight against poverty in Africa gives me energy. It gives me hope to see someone prominent use his fame to speak up for those who are often neglected. The ONE campaign that Bono started shows that if everyone does his/her part, we can make a difference.

Gabriela Mistral: This Nobel Prize-winning poet from Chile has written a powerful poem, *His Name is Today.*[xii] She emphasizes that the child cannot wait for tomorrow to be cared for – the child's name is "Today." It reminds me that we must fight for justice for children today – so many children's lives depend on it.

Anne Weems: She was a gifted Presbyterian poet. I had the privilege of attending college with her. Her poems have touched my heart and she is able to put into words much more eloquently many of my emotions. Two of my favorite poems are *Feed My Sheep* and *I See Your Pain.* [xiii]

FEED MY SHEEP
Jesus said, "Feed my sheep."
There were no conditions:
Least of all, Feed my sheep if they deserve it.
Feed my sheep if you feel like it.
Feed my sheep if you have any leftovers.
Feed my sheep if the mood strikes you.
if the economy's OK . . .
if you're not too busy . . .
No conditions . . just, "Feed my sheep."
Could it be that God's Kingdom will come
when each lamb is fed?
We who have agreed to keep covenant
are called to feed the sheep
even when it means the grazing will be done
on our own front lawns.

I SEE YOUR PAIN
I see your pain
        and want to banish it
        with a wave of a star,
but have no star.

I see your tears
    and want to dry them
     with the hem of an angel's gown,
but have no angel.
I see your heart fallen to the ground
    and want to return it
     wrapped in cloths woven of rainbow,
but have no rainbow.
God is the One
    who has stars, and angels and rainbows,
and I am the one
 God sends to sit beside you
  until the stars come out
   and the angels dry your tears
    and your heart is back in place,
     rainbow blessed.

End Notes

i. This was also the year that the Presbyterian Church in the United States (PCUS) in the south and the United Presbyterian Church in the United States of America (UPCUSA) in the north voted to merge and form a new denomination, the Presbyterian Church (USA). It took several years, however, to complete the merger.

ii. Mustached guenons are capable of jumping sixty-five feet. See neprimateconservancy.org

iii. Mirabai Starr, The Showings of Julian of Norwich, A New Translation (2013) "Showing of Love," page 77.

iv. Searching for Shalom: Resources for Creative Worship, by Anne Weems, Westminster John Knox Press (1981), page 47.

v. The Hope Factor: Engaging the Church in the HIV-AIDS Crisis, edited by Tetsunao Yamamori, David Dageforde, and Tina Bruner. World Vision, 2003.

vi. UNAIDS. December 1999. Update on the global HIV/AIDS epidemic. Accessed from: http://data.unaids.org/pub/report/2000/2000_gr_en.pdf

vii. Interesting paper on this topic: Case et al. Orphans in Africa: Parental Death, Poverty, and School Enrollment. Demography, Volume 41-Number 3, August 2004: 483–508. http://www.princeton.edu/~accase/downloads/Orphans_in_Africa.pdf

viii. https://www.state.gov/about-us-pepfar/

ix. To access most recent (2018) progress to benchmarks in HIV treatment in several African countries, including Zambia and Zimbabwe: (1) UNAIDS 2018 Reference Data. https://www.unaids.org/sites/default/files/media_asset/unaids-data-2018_en.pdf

(2) Population-Based HIV Impact Assessment. https://zw.usembassy.gov/wp-content/uploads/sites/178/PEPFAR-Fact-

Sheet_PHIA_FINAL.pdf

x. The World Bank. Life expectancy in years (total) – Zimbabwe. Accessed from: https://data.worldbank.org/indicator/SP.DYN.LE00.IN?locations=ZW

xi. Do it Anyway, by Mother Teresa.

xii. His Name is Today, by Gabriela Mistral.

xiii. Searching for Shalom: Resources for Creative Worship, by Anne Weems, Westminster John Knox Press (1981), page 47 and page 88.

About the Author

Nancy Wooddell Warlick grew up in West Virginia. She knew from a young age that God was calling her to become a missionary, and specifically to become a missionary in what was then the Belgian Congo. With her husband, Bill Warlick, she served as a Presbyterian mission worker based in the Democratic Republic of Congo (renamed Zaire in 1971) and later in Zimbabwe, living out her calling in a number of African countries. Nancy became a witness before the U.S. Senate Foreign Relations Committee to the crisis unfolding in Zaire. From hilarious family adventures with her three children to heart-warming and heart-breaking tales of vulnerable children on the streets of Africa, she looks back on a life of joy, serving the God she loves. Nancy and Bill are retired and live in her family home in Florida, where they stay in touch with their African brothers and sisters and enjoy keeping up with their children and grandchildren. Nancy has been an active member of Bread for the World for over 40 years and continues advocating for children and the vulnerable in the U.S. and in Africa.

Three Generations of Warlicks – July 2005. Bottom row (L-R): Shamba, William, Kathy, Chloe (on Kathy's lap), Frances. Top row (L-R): Robert, Elizabeth, Bill, Jack (on Bill's lap), Me, Dan

What others are saying about *Adventures in Faith*

"Anyone who knows Nancy Warlick—and those who don't—will find this no-frills, straight-from-the-heart report of her ADVENTURES in Africa a motivation to self-giving, Christ-like love no matter where you live. Her engagement with African children is especially compelling."
—Rev. Art Simon, Founder and president emeritus of Bread for the World

"Missionary Nancy Warlick has written a fascinating and inspirational book about a lifetime career centered around mission in sub-Saharan Africa, and the impressive role of Nancy Warlick in the center of that story. I had the privilege of working closely with Nancy in various "chapters" of that story and am grateful for the many ways that the Holy Spirit working through Nancy was able to stand up to "principalities and powers" (as was the case in the Congo and Zimbabwe) and to show forth a heart of love and compassion through so many ministries in country after country in Southern Africa. Reading this book will renew your passion for God's work around the world, and I recommend it to you."
—Rev. Dr. Clifton Kirkpatrick, Stated Clerk Emeritus Presbyterian Church (USA)

"I have heard it said that when Nancy Warlick arrived in a place the dictators shuddered, and the children rejoiced. This story of her life and faith is filled with the stories of African Christians whom she and Bill met during their years there. This remarkable book will be an encouragement to your faith and a call to action wherever God has placed you on his mission field."
—Rev. Dr. Rob Weingartner, Executive Director of The Outreach Foundation 2002 – 2020.

"One of the greatest challenges for humanity is that the human story on the African continent has not always been told with the compassion and hope-inspiring honesty it deserves. A lot of the good work of God in Africa remains narrated within oral tradition, so it is great that Nancy has taken time to tell of God's goodness witnessed as she and Bill faithfully followed God in Africa and beyond. One really gets the impression that both Nancy and her husband Bill are God's children of Africa born and raised offshore to take advantage of freedoms and resources so that they could serve Africa effectively.

To me, Nancy's personal contribution is best embraced in the way she literally sat, talked, and encouraged my wife Lydia as she was in hospital to give birth to one of our sons. Lydia was in labour for too many hours, and Nancy's presence and gentle reading of Bible verses were a much-appreciated accompaniment. In many ways, Africa is in labour for too many hours and needs people like Nancy and Bill to accompany, advocate, and encourage towards the birth of new signs of the kingdom of God on a troubled continent. Nancy and Bill accompanied and encouraged many individuals, churches, and communities in Africa as they endured labour in the birth of new Godly dreams, structures, and realities. This book gives a glimpse into what God was able to do as they served faithfully. It gives a vision towards other great possibilities not only in Africa but in the world as well."
—Rev. Paul Neshangwe, Pastor and leader in the Presbyterian Church in Zimbabwe